Betty in the Sky
with a Suitcase

Betty N. Thesky

With Janet Spencer, Trivia Queen

RIVERBEND
PUBLISHING

Dedication

*I dedicate this book to all the flight attendants and pilots
who generously shared their stories with me. I'm privileged to know
and work with such fabulously entertaining professionals!*

Acknowledgments

I want to thank Nanette Weston, who took the time out of her busy schedule to draw cartoons. The cartoon on the front cover is actually one she drew of me when I first started flying…and I still love it!

I would like to thank my parents who, if they were still with us, would have loved the fact that I have a book.

Thanks to Danielle Richie for being so sweet to help vector the cartoons on short notice. Thanks to Robert, Christy and Maria for the much needed advice along the way.

A big thanks to Janet's husband Jerry for listening to my podcast and telling Janet about me, and of course a huge thanks to Janet Spencer because without her there wouldn't be a book at all!

I owe a huge debt of thanks to all the podcast listeners who found my show, listened for years and told others about it! Since I never did any advertising or marketing the popularity was truly built from their word of mouth.

And finally I would like to thank Joe d'Eon for inspiring me to start podcasting!

Betty in the Sky with a Suitcase
Copyright © 2010 by Betty N. Thesky
Published by Riverbend Publishing, Helena, Montana

ISBN 13: 978-1-60639-011-5

Printed in the United States of America.

1 2 3   4 5 6 7 8 9 SB 16 15 14 13 12 11 10

Cover design by Bob Smith
Text design by Barbara Fifer
Logo design by Nanette Weston

Riverbend Publishing
P.O. Box 5833
Helena, MT 59604
1-866-787-2363
www.riverbendpublishing.com

Contents

••• I'm only going to fly for 2 years

• • • • • I said the same thing 46 years ago?!

Hi, I'm Betty...

I work as a flight attendant for a major airline. I grew up in a small town outside of Pittsburgh, Pennsylvania. From the time I was a little girl I knew I wanted to get out of that small town to see and do everything the world had to offer.

Because my family didn't have a lot of money and I was intent on traveling around the world, I decided a job with the airlines would give me the freedom and opportunities to follow my dreams.

When I first started flying, I was fascinated by the stories the senior flight attendants would tell. So much can happen when you trap hundreds of people in a metal tube streaming across the sky. Most of the traveling public probably never see past the uniforms to discover what a diverse, educated and entertaining group airline employees can be. For years I had a nagging urge to share these stories.

Then in 2006 I met Joe d'Eon. Joe is an airline captain who started the podcast called "Fly With Me" at FlyWithJoe.com. Joe started podcasting at the virtual onset of this new media outlet. A podcast is like a radio show people can listen to on their computer or iPod. I met Joe on the crew van driving to the airport in Maui. On our way to work, Joe had his recorder and microphone out and was asking us for funny stories. So during our flight back to the mainland, once our service was completed of course, I high-tailed it up to the cockpit and told countless stories. I love old fashioned story-telling, and if you put a microphone in front of me, I'm off to the races!

As luck would have it, I flew with Joe again and he suggested

I get my own microphone and recorder and become a correspondent for his show. I went out and purchased the equipment and began recording stories. Well, let's just say my enthusiasm really outweighed my technical expertise. I had no idea how to edit audio content! As a result, the material I sent Joe was less than ideal. The ever gracious Joe politely suggested that maybe I should do my own show.

That was the humble beginning of my podcast show called "Betty in the Sky with a Suitcase" at BettyInTheSky.com. I'm amazed anyone listened to those early podcasts! I was so ill equipped to produce a show that the first couple of episodes were in mono. But with help from Joe and my faithful listeners, I managed to get the hang of it and now my show has an audience of 578,000 listeners!

Because of the popularity of my podcast, Janet "The Trivia Queen" Spencer approached me with this book project. Some of the stories I've included were sent to me by listeners. If you would like be included in a future "Betty in the Sky with a Suitcase" book, you can send stories to BettyInTheSky@gmail.com. If your story is selected, I will send you an autographed copy of the book.

I never expected to have a book published. It just goes to show that you should always follow your dreams, aim for the sky, and remember to enjoy the ride!

Pranks,
Practical Jokes, &
General Leg-Pulling

*Years ago it was a real coup to get a job with the
airlines. Therefore, we airline employees knew we had
it pretty good. So once the duties were done, the mood
was generally pretty light. We enjoyed playing jokes and
pranks on each other and usually the passengers
never knew what was going on!*

Betty:

"Once on a long full flight to Honolulu, I was chatting with the
captain and co-pilot in the cockpit when the co-pilot described
something he'd seen flight attendants do to entertain themselves
on the ground or on flights with no passengers. It involved tucking
the tail end of a toilet paper roll down the lavatory, unwinding
the toilet paper the length of the plane, then flushing. The pow-
erful suction of the lav would suck the toilet paper down, like
a kid slurping spaghetti. Well, the captain just had to see this in

action, even though we had a completely full flight. He told me to go set everything up and call him when it was ready. I got one fellow flight attendant to guard the door to the lav in the back of the plane while I walked backwards up the aisle, unrolling toilet paper as I went. It must have looked outrageously insane to the passengers, but it was, after all, a long flight in the middle of the day to a vacation destination, so I figured everyone would be willing to play along. I just kept telling people, 'It's an experiment!' and that piqued their interest. When the toilet paper was laid out the length of the plane, I called the captain, and when he stepped out of the cockpit, I gave the thumbs-up signal to my accomplice in the back, and she pushed the flush button. Well, that piece of toilet paper lifted into the air, waved like a noodle, and SCHWOOSH! went down the lav. The entire plane erupted into applause and cheers, and the captain said it was the neatest trick he'd ever seen on a plane."

A pilot:

"I was working for an airline that had installed a kind of a dash-cam or web-cam in the cockpit. It was focused on the instrument panel, showing only the panels and the hands of the pilots. This was so passengers could see what was going on in the cockpit during takeoff and landing. Well, one pilot who was something of a joker smuggled the arm and hand of a gorilla suit on board. When the flight was ready for takeoff, the passengers were treated to the sight of the co-pilot's hand holding a banana in front of the instrument panel. Then a giant gorilla hand reached out to take the banana and push the throttle forward. I believe the dash-cams were phased out quite quickly following that incident."

Around 25% of first class passengers are paying full fare. The rest are…

A pilot:

"A pilot I know who used to fly a DC-3 would shake things up on his flights by always carrying a bucket full of loose nuts and bolts. Whenever the plane would hit turbulence, he would take a handful of nuts and bolts and roll them down the aisle of the plane, and then send the co-pilot out with a wrench in one hand and a screwdriver in the other hand asking the passengers, 'Excuse me, did you see some airplane parts come by here just now? I need those!' The prank never failed to get a rise out of the passengers!"

A pilot:

"A pilot friend of mine named Vern is a real practical joker and loves to put one over on you. He flew regularly with another pilot named Jake, who was dubbed 'shaky Jake' because he was always nervous and jumpy. One day, Vern and the flight engineer decided to target Jake. Vern went to the maintenance shop at the airport and sorted through the trash till he found a big black plug that was full of wires. He took this to the plane and, before Shaky Jake arrived, he stuck that thing up under the dash near the rudder pedals, where it could be seen without interfering with anything. When Shaky Jake arrived, he looked at that mess of wires down there and said, 'What's that? What is that thing?' Vern and the flight engineer just shrugged and said they didn't know. They took off, and every so often, Shaky Jake looked down at that mysterious black-wired thing and wondered what it was. Finally he couldn't contain himself any more, so he reached down and grabbed it and yanked it out. At the same moment, the flight engineer threw a whole bunch of switches so lights started flashing all over the instrument panel. Immediately Shaky Jake started screaming, 'Oh my God! We're gonna crash!' and he didn't stop hollering until Vern and the flight engineer started laughing their butts off. No harm was done, but I doubt if it made Shaky Jake any less shaky."

A male flight attendant:
"Everyone knows that at the beginning of the flight, the flight attendants have to walk through a safety demo. Part of that demo involves holding up the safety information card which has emergency procedures written on it. There's one in every pocket in every seat, so people can see where the emergency exits are and so forth. The flight attendants doing the safety demo holds this card up high in the air so passengers will recognize it in their seat pockets. But what I didn't know on this particular day was that someone had grabbed the safety information card I use for my demo and written, 'I LOVE SEX' in magic marker on the inside of the card, so when I held it above my head and opened it up, it was like a big billboard. There I was, standing in front of a plane full of passengers, holding up a sign that said, 'I LOVE SEX' and wondering why everyone started laughing and clapping. I was very popular on that flight."

A pilot:
"We had a new flight attendant on board, and as a practical joke we decided to initiate her by having her page a passenger. We handed her a boarding pass with a name on it and asked her to get on the PA system and ask for that person to come forward. The name on the boarding pass was 'Anita Mann' and she was perfectly happy to announce: 'Anita Mann, please ring your call button.' I have no idea how many men answered that call."

A flight attendant:

"Back in the days before rules prohibiting sexual-harassment awareness made such games dangerous, I heard of one pilot who cooked up a scheme. He brought a dozen roses on board and kept the bouquet in the cockpit with him. During the flight, he called the flight attendants to the cockpit one at a time, beginning with whoever had the most seniority. He would chat with her a while, and before long, she would ask what the roses were for. He'd reply that they could be hers if she would smooch everyone in the cockpit. Of course, she'd get all offended and leave—without the roses. Then the next flight attendant would be called up, with the same results. Finally the newest flight attendant on board would be summoned to the cockpit, and when she inevitably asked about the roses, the pilot would say, 'Well, I knew there was a new hire on board, so I bought these roses just for you. Welcome to the team!' and she would proudly walk out of the cockpit with the roses—and then would have no idea why everyone else on board treated her like she was some kind of hussy."

An engineer:

"It was my first flight as an engineer and there were a bunch of senior flight attendants on board. When they found out it was my first time as engineer they spent the entire flight going out of their way to make me feel welcome—catering to me, pandering to me, cracking jokes about me, and it was a wonderful, light-hearted flight. When we arrived at our destination, they all hurried off the plane, but I still had to get my gear together. I was hurrying to catch up with them, but when I went to put my jacket on, I couldn't get my hands through the sleeves. They had sewn the sleeves together. I finally punched my arms through the sleeves and went to button it up, but they had sewn the button

---

holes closed. I went to put on my cap not knowing that it was full of baby powder. And as I made my way through the airport I discovered my wings were upside-down and my name tag was attached to the back of my collar. Well, the next morning I was all put back together again and heading to my next flight when I ran into one of those attendants. She gave me a hug and told me I'd been a real trouper about putting up with their pranks. Then she said, 'Oh, you have a little something on your collar' and she brushed it off for me. I didn't think a thing of it until I reached my plane and discovered that when she was supposedly brushing something off my starched white collar, she was really marking it up with blood-red lipstick. I had walked clear through the airport like that. And I had to go on the next flight like that. And then had to go home to my wife like that."

A pilot:

"It was one of my first trips in my new job as an engineer on a 727. Halfway through the flight, a flight attendant came to the cockpit door and said she was in contact with Ops and had been informed that the entire crew had to submit urine samples to be tested for drugs as soon as we arrived at our destination. A few minutes later, the pilot got up and went to the lav and came back with a cup full of his 'sample.' Then the co-pilot did the same. They indicated that it was now my turn, but I thought they were pretty dumb for peeing into a cup with no lid, and since I'm smarter than that, I peed into a bottle with a screw-on cap. When I returned to the cockpit with this, the pilot and co-pilot launched into a tirade about the company's drug testing policies. They got so worked up about it that they both declared they were not going to submit to the drug test—and they upended their cups and drank the contents down in one gulp. That's when

About 47% of all frequent flyer miles are earned on the ground.

I knew I'd been had. Their cups were full of apple juice. My bottle wasn't."

Betty:

"During a period when things were not going well in the airline industry, everyone was depressed and flying had become discouraging. I decided I needed to do something to lighten things up. At an airport shop I bought a little white wind-up mouse and began to take it with me wherever I went. When a pilot stepped out of the cockpit on the way to the lav, or when a fellow flight attendant was standing in the galley, I'll secretly let this wind-up mouse go and watch the fun. They would scream, jump up on seats, and when they realized it's a toy, they'd laugh. It never failed to lighten the mood. Once I was flying with a flight attendant who was a very sweet and pretty. She had already been victimized by the wind-up mouse and was familiar with the joke. On the same flight a brand new flight attendant was on board. After we

Your attention, please.

Public announcements collected from *The Plane Truth: Shift Happens at 35,000 Feet* by A. Frank Steward:

"There may be 50 ways to leave your lover, but there are only six ways to leave this airplane."

"Should the cabin lose pressure, hopefully oxygen masks will drop from the overhead compartment. Please place the bag over your mouth and nose before assisting children, or other adults acting like children."

"We've reached cruising altitude and will be turning down the cabin lights for your comfort and to enhance the appearance of your flight attendants and the meal choice today."

"If you need direction during the flight, a flight attendant would be more than happy to tell you where to go."

Approximately 75% of all frequent flyer miles are never redeemed.

"For our meal selection, we have the choice of the brown meaty gook or the white stuff with yellowish sauce."

"The only place to smoke on today's flight is on the wing. Please step through, feet first, and follow the arrows. If you can light 'em, you can smoke 'em."

"If you are seated in an exit row seat and are unable to perform the exit row duties, please ask a flight attendant to reseat you. If you are unwilling to perform the exit row duties, the captain will be back to discuss your attitude."

"Thank you for flying with us today. The next time you get the inclination to blast through the skies in a pressurized metal tube, carrying approximately 50,000 pounds of flammable liquid, we hope you will think of us again."

finished with our service and had a moment to ourselves, this new hire walked up to my sweet, pretty friend and started complaining about how all the experienced flight attendants kept picking on her and playing pranks and practical jokes just because she was new. She was pouting and sulking over this treat-

ment and my friend put her arm around her shoulders and sincerely commiserated, saying, 'Yes, you poor thing, I know just how mean those senior flight attendants can be. Isn't it terrible?' And then with her arm still around the poor thing, she turned her head to me and secretly hissed, 'Get the mouse!' So I got the mouse and let it go on the galley floor. Well, it was a great show and there were arms flying every direction, and plenty of screaming, too. But

Around 12 million free tickets are issued annually due to frequent flyer miles.

I'll never forget the image of this young pretty flight attendant, acting so sympathetic to the plight of this innocent new hire, while simultaneously whispering, 'Get the mouse!'

A passenger:

"I was stranded in Phoenix one night when a connecting flight was grounded due to fog at our home airport. About a hundred passengers were milling around the gate area, waiting to fly standby to anywhere that would get them closer to home. A gate agent got on the PA offering a $150 travel voucher to anyone who would bump themselves from the only flight going to Kansas that night. You should have heard the ripple go through the crowd when a prisoner, escorted by a couple of cops, suddenly thrust both handcuffed arms in the air and shouted, 'I'll take the deal!' "

A military pilot:

"An Air Force captain who was a friend of mine was flying a 141 out of Fort Benning, Georgia. He was flying the plane for the paratroopers who were taking training jumps out of the back. Besides the paratroopers, the plane also carried a couple of loadmasters, who were in charge of loading the plane and getting the paratroopers out of the door when it was their turn to jump. Because loadmasters are always near the open doors of the plane, they were required to wear reserve parachutes just in case something should happen. Well, the paratroopers thought it was funny to grab the loadmasters and throw them out of the plane as the last paratroopers were jumping out. Needless to say, the loadmasters didn't find this funny at all but it happened several times. They tried the normal channels to stop these hijinks but that didn't work. So they came up with a scheme.

The average number of people airborne over the U.S. at any moment is 61,000.

It was the middle of summer. The flight was hot, muggy, and bumpy. About 140 paratroopers were crammed elbow-to-elbow on the benches. Then the captain started deliberately fish-tailing the airplane, so everyone got a little queasy. One of the loadmasters started acting like he was about to barf and made a mad dash for the lavatory in the front of the plane. While he was out of sight, he took out a baggie full of warm vegetable soup that he had hidden in his uniform. He made noises as if he was vomiting, then stepped out of the lavatory, looking very grim, and holding the brown, liquid-filled baggy.

The loadmaster handed the baggie to the paratrooper at the head of the row and said to pass it back to the loadmaster at the end of the plane to throw out the open door. So there went the warm bag of "vomit," hand to hand down the line of queasy paratroopers, to the rear loadmaster.

With everybody watching him, the loadmaster at the back of the plane looked at the baggie, opened it, sniffed it, and then drank it all down in one gulp. At that point about half of the paratroopers barfed into their helmets. When they got to the drop zone, everyone was so sick that nobody jumped. They landed back at Fort Benning with a full plane, which was really disgraceful. The captain came back to the paratroopers, who were still completely green around the gills, and said, 'This is going to keep on happening to you until my loadmasters stop getting thrown out of the plane.' End of problem."

A pilot:

"Sometimes when troops are picked up after a long patrol or a tough operation, the loadmaster will offer them some special in-flight catering in the form of cold cans of beer. It's strictly against the rules of course, but the soldiers only get a couple of cans each and they appreciate it. Then the loadmaster makes a show of taking more beer up to the flight deck. The crew will also have gathered some empties and hidden them on the flight deck. After a few minutes, the pilots toss one of these empties out of the cockpit. A minute or two later, another one comes rolling back, and then another. The loadmaster 'tut-tuts' disapprovingly as he clears up the constant flow of empty beer cans. The troops start to get a bit worried. In a little while, after more empties sail out of the cockpit, the pilots deliberately start to roll and pitch the plane. It doesn't take long before one of the soldiers pulls the loadmaster aside and says 'Don't you think they've had enough to drink?!' "

A pilot:

"For seven years I flew C130 Hercules transport aircraft for the Royal Air Force. The Hercules is fairly basic and sparse inside; it's basically just a metal tube with canvas bench seats for our passengers. We really cram soldiers into the aircraft, and when it's full there are four rows of bench seats with soldiers facing each other, knee to knee. Once the engines are running, you can only talk to the person next to you if you shout. Sometimes, once the aircraft is fully loaded with passengers, and while we're waiting to start engines, the flight engineer will make his way from the cockpit down to the back of the aircraft. Of course this involves practically climbing over the passengers to get there, so they can't fail to notice him. When he gets to the back, he opens up the emergency escape hatch, which is a sort of porthole in the roof of the aircraft, and climbs out on top of the aircraft. A couple of minutes later the engines are started and the loadmaster makes a show of noticing the open hatch and closing it. It's now impossible for the passengers to get up and speak to the loadmaster, and before long we take off. Of course, what they don't know is that there is another escape hatch in the roof of the cockpit, and the flight engineer has climbed back in there. The flight proceeds as normal, but once we land, the flight engineer messes up his hair, maybe pours a cup of water over himself, and rumples himself up. As soon as the aircraft reaches its parking spot, the flight engineer climbs out of the cockpit hatch and makes his way down to the back of the aircraft. The crew gives him a minute to get there, then they shut down the engines. As the noise from the propellers dies away, the passengers hear a frantic banging noise. The loadmaster climbs up and opens the hatch at the back of the aircraft where a very shaken, unsteady flight engineer climbs inside and makes his way up to the cockpit, trying all the while not to crack up with laughter!"

Betty:

"I really enjoy traveling all over the planet, but one place I always wanted to go—especially after having read a book about it—was Easter Island. It took quite a bit of arranging, especially since planes land there only every few days, but I finally made it, and the trip was really worth it. The island had a magical feel, not only because

---

the volcanic rocks are magnetic, but also because the famous Moai statues trigger a lot of emotions. Well, I collect vintage stewardess outfits and I took a classic 1970s outfit with me on this trip. I got on a bus tour of the Moai. At one stop, I dashed into the bathroom and changed into this outrageous costume, including gloves, pantyhose, and hat. Well, the entire tour bus was full of native Chileans and when I appeared wearing this outfit, they first looked at me like I was completely nuts. But then they started laughing, and in the end, they all took my picture."

A pilot:

"One of the practical jokes we pull on new flight attendants is to hand them a garbage bag and tell them to go take an air sample for us, because the air conditioning technicians are concerned about allergens or contami-

Surprise!

Marsha Marks, in her book Flying by the Seat of My Pants, *tells about the time a practical joke went awry: "We'd climb into an overhead bin before people boarded and then jump out at unsuspecting passengers as they opened the bin to store their luggage. We played this joke on newly hired flight attendants and pilots stowing luggage for their first check ride. One day I had just climbed into the overhead bin at 37C because the brother of my fellow flight attendant would be traveling with us, and she wanted to 'surprise' him. The door hadn't been snapped shut for more than one minute when I heard tapping and a stage whisper, 'Marsha, get out of the bin! Get out of the bin now!' Then the bin door opened and I yelled, 'Gotcha!' No one moved. I was facing three Secret Service men—not the flight attendant's brother—who were now talking furiously into their wrists. Hey, how could I know that former president Gerald Ford was traveling first class on our flight that day? It was a long time before we ever played the overhead bin joke again."*

Airplanes take off and land every 37 seconds
at O'Hare Airport.

nants. They walk up and down the aisles filling the bag with air, then tying it off so it can be delivered to the lab."

A female flight attendant:

"I was on a flight that had several legs. We were preparing for our fifth or sixth leg of the trip, and we had two legs left. I looked down at my nylons, and I noticed I had a run in my stocking. So I said to the other flight attendant, 'I need to go change my nylons!' and she said, 'What? For two lousy legs?' and I replied, 'Well, I don't think my legs are lousy!'"

A pilot:

"A favorite prank of Air Force pilots, which crews have been playing for years, on all sorts of aircraft, is when a pilot emerges from the cockpit, walking backwards very slowly, carefully unwinding two balls of string. When he gets to the first passenger, he tells him in a loud voice that he has to go back to the toilet and so the passenger should hold on to these two bits of string, keep them tight and try not to pull them. Then the pilot quickly walks off before the passenger can say anything. Of course, the string isn't really attached to the flight controls; the flight engineer is holding the other end of them. But the passenger doesn't know that. To start with, they'll hold them very still, but usually after a minute or two of nothing happening, the passenger will carefully give one string a gentle tug. The flight engineer will feel this and tell the co-pilot, who will bank the aircraft fairly sharply in that direction. The engineer usually feels an immediate corresponding tug on the opposite bit of string and then nothing further as the passenger is now convinced he is flying the aircraft! After a few minutes, the pilot comes back from the toilet, thanks the passenger for doing such a great job, and carefully takes the bits of string back."

More hot dogs are sold at Chicago's O'Hare Airport than at any other location on the planet—2 million annually.

Betty:

"Every job has aspects that are boring and repetitive. For flight attendants, it's saying 'hello' three hundred times when passengers board, and then 'good-bye' three hundred more times when they disembark. One flight attendant I know said that he could probably say anything at all as people deplaned and, as long as he was smiling, no one would ever even notice. So the next time we landed, he bade people farewell by saying, 'Neeboop! Loonup! Felspit!' while continuously smiling and nodding. No one noticed or, if they did, no one mentioned anything. And the thing about it was that his good-bye smile was bigger than ever before!"

At peak periods, controllers at O'Hare Airport handle 210 flights per hour.

Beverage
Boo-Boos

*"Can I get you something to drink?" You would think
that must be one of the simplest questions you can ask a
person. Well, that's the beauty of the traveling public...
they always surprise you!*

Betty:

"One of the things that really irritates flight attendants are
headphones, especially when people refuse to take them off
when you're trying to talk to them. Both the noise-canceling
headphones and loud music headphones can completely cut
off communication when a flight attendant is trying to serve a
passenger and it makes the situation much more difficult than
it needs to be. One day I was trying to serve drinks to a man
wearing noise-canceling headphones but he couldn't hear me
and I couldn't get his attention. So I was joking with the other
passengers, saying, 'I could say anything in the world to him right
now and he wouldn't hear me.' But they cautioned me, saying he
might be able to read my lips. So I started thinking up things I

could say that would look like I was saying, 'something to drink?' Then I leaned over to him and said, 'Do you need a shrink?' and he said, 'Diet Coke!' Well, everyone laughed (except for the guy who was still completely oblivious) so I continued on down the aisle, now looking forward to serving someone else with headphones. To the next person wearing headphones I said, 'Are your toe nails pink?' and he replied, 'Just water!' Now I enjoy meeting people who are worlds away underneath their headphones, because I can ask them if their feet stink and hand them a cranapple juice with a big smile on my face."

A flight attendant:

"I asked one lady if she would like something to drink, and she replied that she would love some tea. I asked her, 'How do you take your tea?' meaning, with sugar, cream, or lemon, but she looked at me blankly and replied, 'In a cup!'"

Betty:

"We serve plenty of coffee on every flight, but flight attendants also drink lots of coffee themselves, especially since we're often short on sleep or flying at odd hours. On one extremely early morning flight I was sipping my own coffee while also serving pre-departure drinks for the passengers. I always drink my coffee with creamer and a sweetener. Well, I was still pretty bleary when a first class passenger asked for coffee with cream but no sugar. I served him, and a few moments later went to sip my own cup of coffee. I was perplexed because suddenly my coffee wasn't sweet any more, and I had already drunk half of it. Suddenly with a sinking feeling I knew I had accidentally served my coffee to the man in first class. I looked and sure enough, I could see my lipstick marks on the side of the cup. He hadn't yet taken a sip of

There are about 171 miles (274 km) of wiring inside a Boeing 747.

the coffee and hadn't noticed the lipstick, so I hurried over and grabbed the cup right out of his hand just as he was about to lift it to his lips. I said, 'You know what? That cup was the bottom of a pot, and we just made a fresh pot, so let me take this one and I'll be right back with a better cup of coffee for you.' I got back to the galley and heaved a huge sigh of relief. That close call woke me up more than the coffee did."

A flight attendant:

"One of the things we really hate is accidentally spilling something on one of the passengers. One flight attendant accidentally spilled tomato juice on the expensive white pants of a lady in first class. She was horrified at what she had done, and asked the passenger if she had a spare pair of pants to change into while she made it her mission to get the tomato juice out of the pants. When the lady changed, the flight attendant took those pants into the lav and used club soda and hand soap to scrub them till they were white again. But then they were soaking wet, and she didn't want to hand sopping pants back to the lady. So she turned on the galley oven, opened the oven door, draped the pants over a coat hanger, and hung the pants to dry

> ### Cola Wars
> *Frank Steward, in his book* The Plane Truth: Shift Happens at 35,000 Feet, *tells of the time he offered a first-class passenger a drink:* "What can I get you to drink?" I asked. "A Coke, please," the businessman responded. We no longer served Coke and I was tired of the question, "Is Pepsi all right?" so I merely handed him a Pepsi. "I'm sorry; I asked for a Coke." "Same thing," I replied, trying to be cute. I couldn't quite understand why this man went into a fit, until I found out that he was vice president of Coca-Cola.

The wings on a Boeing 747 cover an area a little larger than a basketball court.

in the rising heat. Then she got called away to serve other passengers, and by the time she got back to the galley to check on the pants, the heat was melting a hole in them. So now she had to go give the lady her pants with a three-inch hole, but hey—at least the tomato juice was out!"

A flight attendant:

"When I was newly hired I was a lot slower at beverage service than the more experienced flight attendants on the crew. Back then we would fill a bin with beverages and then put it on top of our cart. Well, I was in a real hurry so I put the bin on top of the jumpseat just for a minute before transferring it to my cart, and then I went to get something out of the bottom of the jumpseat. I had forgotten that when you pull the bottom of the jumpseat out, the top of the jumpseat flattens—so that entire bin of beverages tipped over and landed right on top of the head of the lady sitting behind it. All kinds of juice and soda pop went streaming all down her face, soaking her hair. I was mortified and humiliated, but instead of getting mad about it she just said, 'Don't you worry about it, honey! It's a wig!' and she pulled her wig off her head, shook out the juice, and put it back on her head, saying, 'See? It's wash-and-wear hair! No harm done!'"

> ### Do you have change for a hundred?
> A. Frank Steward in his book The Plane Truth: Shift Happens at 35,000 Feet *tells it like it is:* "Ninety-nine percent of flight attendants who are handed a hundred-dollar bill for a four-dollar drink despise you and your attempt to get a free drink. Eight out of ten will actually try to collect the change, just to spite you. I now carry 97 one-dollar bills as a way of countering such attempts."

The #1 requested in-flight drink? Bottled water, which recently surpassed cola.

A flight attendant:

"I was doing beverage service in first class and was serving a man who was seated next to his girlfriend. When I asked him what he wanted to drink he said, 'Do you have apple juice?' and I said, 'I do!' He said, 'Do you have cranberry juice?' and I said, 'I do!' He said, 'Do you have Bloody Mary mix?' and I said, 'I do!' Then he turned to his girlfriend and said, 'See how easy it is to get a flight attendant to say 'I do'?"

Betty:

"I was working a flight with an attendant who tended to be a little bit silly. As we were serving beverages, she handed a passenger a soft drink and then spun around, turning 360 degrees, and then went back to serving more drinks. I said, 'Um, excuse me, but did you just twirl?' and she said yes, and I said, 'Why?' and she just shrugged and said, 'It's fun!' and the passengers in the area all started laughing. Well, it was a long flight at the end of the day, and the mood on the plane had been a little crabby with grumpy passengers and tired children, so we concocted a scheme to use twirling to cheer everyone up. Whenever we're doing beverage service, I serve two rows of passengers and the other flight attendant serves two rows of passengers. When

The flight deck on a Boeing 747 has 365 lights, gauges, and switches.

we're finished serving and are ready to move the beverage cart forward to the next group of passengers, we'll typically say something like, 'ready, Freddy!' Well, we decided that instead of saying something to indicate we were ready to move the cart, we would just twirl instead—I would twirl, then she would twirl, then we would move the cart. This little bit of nonsensical silliness made everyone on the plane laugh, especially us. By the time everyone had received their drinks, mission was accomplished and everyone was in a good mood again."

A flight attendant:

"Sometimes all it takes to make our day is a polite 'please' or 'thank you.' One day a grandmother, daughter, and granddaughter boarded together. As soon as I started drink service the little granddaughter started screaming for a cola, even though she

I wonder how long it will take for the crew to figure out that the kid running up and down the aisle is mine?!

Those beverage service carts the flight attendants push up...

was several rows back. I didn't feel like giving in to her hollering so I continued to serve passengers in the proper order while she continued to yell for a cola. I did my best to ignore her, and wondered why her mother and grandmother weren't using the opportunity to teach her some manners. When I got to the row ahead of her, she was still shouting for a cola. By then I was determined to make her wait her turn. When I served her grandmother, the kid was screaming for a cola. When I served her mother, she was screaming for cola. Finally it was her turn, and as I handed her a drink I said, 'What's the magic word?' She looked at me blankly. Her mother looked at me blankly. Her grandmother looked at me blankly. Then her mother and grandmother turned to me and said simultaneously, '*Abracadabra?*' "

Betty:

"The beverage carts we push up and down the aisles are very heavy and it can hurt a lot when a passenger's elbow or a foot or some fingers accidentally get squished. Because the aisles are so narrow, this is a serious concern. Therefore, I am constantly saying, 'Watch the cart! Watch the cart! Watch the cart!' as I go up and down the aisles, giving people warning. One night on a late flight when I was very tired, and the cabin was dark and the aisle was littered with arms and legs and feet that I needed to navigate around, I walked from the front of the plane all the way to the back saying, 'Watch the cart! Watch the cart!' When I got to the back of the plane, I suddenly realized….I didn't have a cart!' "

...and down the aisles each weigh about 250 lbs (113 kg).

Watch the cart,
watch your elbows,
watch your knees,
watch your toes...
please don't run my
pantyhose!

Total area of Denver International Airport, in square miles: 53 (137 sq/km).
Total area of Manhattan Island, in square miles: 22.4 (58 sq/km).

Roger That!
Control Tower
Comedy

*Maybe it's because of the penguin suit of a uniform or
the military background, but you generally expect pilots
to be serious in nature. But pilots as a whole have really
surprised me. They have all kinds of funny stories. I flew
for many years not knowing all the funny exchanges that
go on between the cockpit and the control tower. Read on
and see for yourself…these guys are funny!*

A pilot:

"A 747 flight was coming into Kennedy Airport when the
air traffic controller needed to open up some space before the
final descent. He directed the pilot to do a 'right 360' which is
a common command and simply means that you do a big circle
in the sky and then get back in line. The pilot got all uppity and
started berating the air traffic controller, saying, 'Do you have
any idea how much it costs in fuel to turn a 747 airplane 360

degrees?' The air traffic controller replied, 'No, I have no idea.' So the pilot hollered back, 'It costs over $400!' The air traffic controller came right back on and said, 'Good! Give me a $400 turn to the right!' "

A pilot:

"Several years ago I overheard this exchange between the control tower in Boston and a commuter plane:

Pilot: Request a direct to Pittsburgh.

Boston Center: Your request for a direct routing is on request, but first, we have a request.

Pilot: OK, what is your request?

Boston Center: Please take an extra-strength Bloody Mary to seat 13C.

Pilot: Boston Center, let me get this straight. Our request for a direct routing is on request, and your request is for an extra-strength Bloody Mary to seat 13C, correct?

Boston Center: That's affirmative.

A few minutes of silence went by.

Pilot: Boston Center, an extra-strong Bloody Mary has been delivered to seat 13C, free of course, as well as an extra bag of peanuts.

Boston Center: Cleared direct Pittsburgh.

Pilot: Boston Center, OK. Who the heck is in seat 13C?

Boston Center: The wife of the controller next me. She is going to Pittsburgh to visit family.

Pilot: Boston Center, tell him she will be well taken care of.

A pilot:

"When I was in the military I was an aircraft commander working with a pilot and we were practicing touch-and-go maneuvers,

---

About 27,000 flights take off each day across the U.S.

which is when you land only to take off again and circle around and land once again. On this day, there was a woman controller in the tower, and she was good. And she knew she was good. The pilot put down his landing gear a tiny bit early—maybe a few seconds sooner than normal—and the controller got on the radio and said, 'Zero Foxtrot Zero One, is there any reason why your wheels are down?' I thought she was being way too picky, so I grabbed the microphone and replied, 'Yes, there is. We have discovered that it tends to cushion the landing considerably!' Everyone in the plane cracked up, and we didn't hear any more criticism from her for the rest of the day."

We'll make it taste like chicken

Tower: *"Eastern 702, cleared for takeoff, contact Departure on frequency 124.7."*

Eastern 702: *"Tower, Eastern 702 switching to Departure. By the way, after we lifted off we saw some kind of dead animal on the far end of the runway."*

Tower: *"Continental 635, cleared for takeoff behind Eastern 702. Did you copy that report from Eastern 702?"*

Continental 635: *"Continental 635, cleared for takeoff, roger; and yes, we copied Eastern…We've already notified our caterers."*

A pilot:

"Germans tend to be very fastidious and punctual and they like everything to be perfect. If you are not doing things the way they think things ought to be done, they will correct you. One day we were taxiing out to a runway in Frankfurt, heading for a runway that was quite a distance away. Ground control cleared a Lufthansa flight to follow the Clipper to Runway 1-A, mean-

About 40 percent of the world's trade goods are carried by air.

ing they were to pull in behind us. Well, the Lufthansa 737 floored it and pulled right out ahead of us, forcing us to slam on the brakes to avoid them. We thought it was because the Lufthansa was on their home ground and they just naturally assumed they would get preferential treatment. Then we heard Ground Control saying, 'Lufthansa, I told you to follow ze Clipper!' and the Lufthansa pilot replied, 'Ve did not see ze Clipper!' There was a short pause, and Ground Control said, 'Roger...' Then Ground Control said to the Lufthansa, 'Turn right at Taxiway Lima...Turn right at Taxiway November...Turn right at Taxiway Papa...Turn right at Taxiway Hotel...' and basically boxed him in behind us. Then Ground Control said, '*Now* do you see ze Clipper?'"

A pilot:

"In Germany a very precise air traffic controller came on the air and asked the Lufthansa pilot if he was familiar with the airport layout. The pilot said no, so the control tower said, 'Turn right at the next intersection!' and the pilot replied, 'Roger!' A few minutes later the control tower said, 'Lufthansa, I told you to turn right!' 'We did turn right!' barked the pilot. 'Well, then,' said the control tower without skipping a beat, 'You're sitting in the cockpit backwards!'"

The windows in an air traffic control tower are always tilted outward...

A co-pilot:

"Radio traffic was really busy when we were trying to takeoff one day; you just couldn't get a word in edgewise. The pilot needed some information, so he asked the tower, 'Do you have a temperature?' The air traffic controller replied, 'No, I don't have a temperature, just a little headache, but thanks for asking!'"

Fill 'er up

An air traffic controller was surprised one day to hear a very calm voice coming from the pilot of a small aircraft saying, "Control Tower, I am out of fuel." The air traffic controller immediately shifted into emergency mode and began spitting instructions: "Reduce air speed! Commence gliding! Do you have the landing strip in sight?" There was a slight pause, followed by the pilot's response: "Um…Tower, I am parked on the south ramp…I just wanted to know where the fuel truck is located."

A co-pilot:

"I was flying with a captain from Houston, a southern country gentleman. Everyone loved him, but one of his quirks was his very slow, deliberate, southern drawl. Well, we were flying up to New York City and he was on the radio to the New York Center. Everyone at the New York Center talks like they're speed reading—very, very fast, rattling off commands so quickly you can hardly catch them. This Texas gent was completely unfazed. He just picked up his radio mike and said in his slow, deliberate Texas drawl, 'New York Center, this is 123. Do you hear how fast I'm talking? Well, that's how fast I listen!' Even New York Center got a chuckle out of that one."

A passenger:

"The German air controllers at Frankfurt Airport are renowned as a short-tempered lot. They not only expect pilots to know gate parking locations, but also how to get there without any assistance

---

…at exactly 15 degrees from vertical in order to reduce reflections.

from them. So it was with some amusement that we listened to the following exchange between Frankfurt ground control and a British Airways 747, call sign Speedbird 206:

Speedbird 206: 'Frankfurt, Speedbird 206! Clear of active runway.'

Ground: 'Speedbird 206. Taxi to gate Alpha One-Seven.'

The Speedbird pulled onto the main taxiway and slowed to a stop.

Ground: 'Speedbird, do you not know where you are going?'

Speedbird 206: 'Stand by, Ground, I'm looking up our gate location now.'

Ground (with arrogant impatience): 'Speedbird 206, have you not been to Frankfurt before?'

Speedbird 206 (coolly): 'Yes, twice in 1944…but I didn't land.' "

Waiting for spares

One day the pilot of a small Cherokee 180 was told by the tower to hold short of the active runway while a large DC-8 landed. The DC-8 landed, rolled out, turned around, and taxied back past the Cherokee. Some quick-witted comedian in the DC-8 crew got on the radio and said, "What a cute little plane. Did you build it all by yourself?" The Cherokee pilot, not about to let the insult go by, came back with a real zinger: "I made it out of DC-8 parts. Another landing like yours and I'll have enough parts for another one!"

A pilot:

"Two aircraft were approaching the same airport at the same moment. One was American Airlines and the other was United. The air traffic controller asked them who wanted to land first since they were both an equal distance from the airport. The American Airline pilot had a date and was in a big hurry to land,

Radio Repartee

Tower: *"Northwest 351, you have traffic at 10 o'clock, 6 miles!"*

Delta 351: *"Give us another hint! We have digital watches!"*

Tower: *"TWA 2341, for noise abatement turn right 45 degrees."*

TWA 2341: *"Center, we are at 35,000 feet. How much noise can we make up here?"*

Tower: *"Sir, have you ever heard the noise a 747 makes when it hits a 727?"*

From an unknown aircraft waiting in a very long takeoff queue:

Unknown aircraft: *"I'm *#!@& bored!"*

Tower: *"Last aircraft transmitting, identify yourself immediately!"*

Unknown aircraft: *"I said I was *#!@& bored, not *#!@& stupid!"*

A DC-10 came in too fast and thus had an exceedingly long roll out after touching down.

San Jose Tower noted: *"American 751, make a hard right turn at the end of the runway, if you are able. If you are not able, take the Guadeloupe exit off Highway 101, make a right at the lights, and return to the airport."*

Control Tower to United 329: *"United 329, your traffic is a Fokker, one o'clock, three miles, eastbound."*

United 329: *"Approach, I've always wanted to say this...I've got the little Fokker in sight."*

...who flew to Casablanca in a Boeing 314 in 1943.

but didn't want to seem rude. So he got on the radio and said, "American, why don't you go first?" The United pilot realized he'd been had."

A pilot:

"There are several models of Fokker airplanes, and their model numbers are keyed to the size of their motors. One captain was instructed by the tower to follow the Fokker down the taxiway, but there were two Fokkers on the tarmac. So the captain radioed the tower asking, 'Do you mean the little motor Fokker or the big motor Fokker?' "

A pilot:

"I was waiting for takeoff when I overheard a radio exchange between another pilot and the tower. The airline had just acquired a number of the new Fokker 100 airplanes, and the guy in the tower was really curious about them. He was asking the Fokker pilot all kinds of questions about the Fokker models. He asked the airline captain how many Fokkers the airline had acquired, and they guy said they'd purchased several dozen so far, but the plane he was piloting was the very first Fokker the airline had purchased. 'No kidding?' said the air traffic controller. 'It's really the very first one?' and the pilot answered, 'Yes. In fact, we call it the Mother.' "

Memorable Moments in Aviation History

1895: "Heavier than air flying machines are impossible."
—Physicist Lord Kelvin

1901: "Flight by machines heavier than air is unpractical and insignificant, if not utterly impossible."—Simon Newcomb

---

What famous pilot flew for 43 years without a pilot's license? Orville Wright.

1903: The first successful flight by Orville and Wilbur Wright occurred at Kitty Hawk when Wilbur flew 852 feet (260 m). The Wright brothers were not the first to fly a plane. Seven years earlier, Samuel Pierpont Langley's 16-foot (4.9 m) plane traveled three quarters of a mile and stayed aloft for a minute and a half. The Wrights' claim to fame was that they made the first flight that carried a human. Langley's plane was unmanned.

"I confess that in 1901, I said to my brother Orville that man would not fly for fifty years….Ever since, I have distrusted myself and avoided all predictions."—Wilbur Wright, 1908

1908: The world's first fatal airplane crash occurred when a propeller broke, sending the aircraft plunging 150 feet (46 m) to earth. The pilot escaped with a broken leg, but the single passenger, Lt. Thomas Selfridge of the U.S. Signal Corps, was killed on impact. The pilot was Orville Wright.

1918: President Wilson and other important officials gathered in May to witness the takeoff of the first airmail flight. The plane was to carry mail from Washington, D.C., to Philadelphia. After takeoff, the plane somehow went off course and landed in Waldorf, Maryland—which is even farther away from Philadelphia than Washington. The mail was eventually delivered by train.

"[Airmail was] an impractical sort of fad, and had no place in the serious job of postal transportation."—Col. Paul Henderson, U.S. 2nd Asst. Postmaster General, 1919

1927: Charles Lindbergh was not the first person to fly across the Atlantic. Dozens of people did that before he did. Lindbergh was the first person to fly nonstop across from New York to Paris. For the 33-hour flight, he took with him only several sandwiches to eat, saying, "If I make it to Paris, I won't need any more; and if I don't make it to Paris, I won't need any more." His flight won him the $25,000 Orteig Prize.

"I decided that if I could fly for ten years before I was killed in a crash, it would be a worthwhile trade for an ordinary lifetime."—Charles Lindbergh in his autobiography, **The Spirit of St. Louis.** He died in 1974 at the age of 72.

The wingspan of a Boeing 747 is longer than the Wright Brothers' first flight.

1938: Howard Hughes filled a compartment on his airplane with ping-pong balls so that it would float if it went down over the ocean. He then proceeded to set the speed record for flying around the world.

1949: A U.S. Superfortress bomber completed the first non-stop flight around the world. The plane traveled 23,452 miles (37,742 km) in 94 hours and 1 minute. It was refueled four times in flight.

1959: John Cook and Bob Timm flew their Cessna 172 in the skies over Las Vegas for 65 days without stopping, setting a record that no one would ever want to break. They 'airlifted' fuel and supplies from a truck that drove down a long straight stretch of highway to match their speed. They covered a distance equal to six times around the world without ever leaving the air space over Vegas. "Next time I feel in the mood to fly endurance, I'm going to lock myself in our garbage can with the vacuum cleaner running. That is, until my psychiatrist opens up for business in the morning," said Cook after the flight.

1986: The Voyager was the first airplane to fly around the world without refueling. Cruising at a speed between 65 and 120 mph (105-193 km/hr) at an altitude of 8,000 to 10,000 feet (2,438-3,048 m), it took pilots Dick Rutan and Jeana Yeager 9 days, 3 minutes and 44 seconds to travel 24,986 miles (40,211 km). The plane used just over 1,000 gallons (3,785 L) of fuel, which weighed nearly 10,000 pounds (4,535 kg). After they landed they found there were still 14 gallons (53 L) of fuel aboard the plane, enough to theoretically travel another 560 miles (901 km) at their regular mileage of 40 miles per gallon (17 km/L).

A Boeing 747 burns about 48 gallons (182 L) of fuel every minute it's airborne.

Lavatory
Laughs

The lavatory is "ripe" with entertainment value.
Who could have guessed there would be so much to make
fun of in an airline bathroom? I just hope these stories
don't all go down the toilet!

A flight attendant:

"I was serving on a flight to L.A. and on that particular plane, the suction on the toilet in the lavatory was extremely strong. We served breakfast, and one lady passenger spilled something on her dress. It was a red silk wrap-around dress, and she went to the bathroom to clean it off. Apparently, she took off the dress in the lavatory, and when she was done cleaning it, she laid it next to the toilet, and then went to the bathroom. When she flushed, a piece of the dress was hanging close enough to the toilet so that it got sucked right in and flushed right down. So there she was, standing there wearing nothing but her underwear. She just stayed in the bathroom until we were ready to land. We started knocking on the door and insisting that she come out and take her seat. She said, 'I cannot come out!' and when we asked why, she opened the door a tiny crack and said, 'My dress got flushed down the toilet!' So one of us loaned her an extra coat so she could come out. When we landed, we explained the situation to the agent and he said, 'Well…do you want your dress back?' and she said emphatically, 'No!' I'm sure that by then her red silk dress was a pretty shade of lavatory blue."

Rocket Science

A flight attendant:

"A male passenger was violently ill in the lav, and he threw up so hard his dentures fell out and got flushed down the toilet. And he wanted them back."

Betty:

"The word spoken most often by a flight attendant is not 'hello' or 'thank you' or 'excuse me' or 'I'm sorry.' The word spoken most often is, 'Push!' That's because the lavatory door is a bi-fold door that opens like a telephone booth. People are always searching for a door knob to try to pull the door open, and they constantly grab the ash tray in the door thinking it must be a handle. So

The first airplane toilets were simply a hole in the fuselage of the plane…

from one end of the flight to the other, the word most often repeated by every flight attendant in America is, 'Push! Push it! Push the door!' because there is always a confused passenger standing in front of the bathroom door trying to figure out how to get in. I think the only professional who uses the word 'push' more than flight attendants must be an obstetrician."

A pilot:

"On one of my flights, a flight attendant answered the call button that was rung from inside one of the lavatories. She responded to the bell and knocked on the bathroom door. A man opened the door.

> ### Pardon my foot
> ### in your underwear
> *Elliot Hester, in his book* Plane Insanity: A Flight Attendant's Tales of Sex, Rage and Queasiness at 30,000 Feet, *recounts the horror story of the pilot of a DC-10 who was flying cross-country on an all-night flight. He stepped out of the cockpit to relieve himself in the first-class lavatory. He opened the door and stepped in, only to be greeted by the outraged screams of a first class passenger who was currently using the facility and who had forgotten to lock the door. The mortified pilot backed out of the bathroom in a hurry, but unfortunately his foot had become tangled in the lady's underwear. Hester describes the scene: "While backing away from the lavatory, the captain inadvertently yanked the woman's legs forward. She screamed again. He tried wiggling his foot out of her panties. She screamed once more. He pulled harder. She screamed louder. He fell on the floor, in full view of the first-class passengers, jiggling his foot like a…like a man with his foot caught in the leg hole of a strange woman's panties. By the time he extricated himself, by the time her panties had snapped back into place and the door had been mercifully shut and locked, the Captain had lost most of his self-esteem and one of his uniform shoes. He retreated into the cockpit and was incommunicado for the entire flight."*

…through which one could see the countryside passing below.

He was seated on the throne and said, 'Could you please bring me a magazine?'"

A flight attendant:

"I was working a flight when the flight engineer stepped out of the cockpit to use the restroom. A lady was in the lavatory but she didn't know how to lock the door, so she was sitting on the throne holding the door closed with her hand. The flight engineer tugged on the door to open it, and she tugged back. He pulled harder, thinking the door was just stuck, and she pulled harder back. Then he gave the door a really hard yank and she came flying out of the bathroom with her pants around her ankles and landed on the floor, right in the middle of the first class aisle!"

Betty:

"In many foreign countries, they don't use the same sort of toilet that we are accustomed to in the U.S. Instead, often there is simply a hole in the ground, with an outline of two feet on either side of the hole. You place your feet on the footprints and squat. And just as we are not accustomed to their squat toilet, they are not used to our sit-down toilet. Sometimes in the lav, people will actually get up and stand on the toilet seat and squat. How do I know this? Two reasons. First, I've seen the footprints on the seat. Second, the same people who are unfamiliar with the use of a flush toilet are often unfamiliar with the way the locking mechanism works on a lavatory door. I've accidentally walked in on them upon occasion. And, upon occasion, other passengers have walked in on them too. They'll rush to me with their eyes wide and say, 'You won't believe what I just saw in the bathroom!' and I'll reply, 'someone was standing on the seat and squatting?' and they say, 'How did you know?!' Well, I've seen it all!"

There's an average of one toilet for every 46 passengers in coach class...

A flight attendant:

"Anyone who has flown on a regular basis knows those little lavatories don't exactly stay as fresh as a daisy. In fact, especially on long flights, they can get downright rank. And the flight attendant's jumpseats are very near the lavatories on almost every aircraft, so nobody knows better than us just how smelly those restrooms can get. That's why many flight attendants tend to carry around some sort of air freshener. On one flight, I was serving with a flight attendant who carried a great big can of aerosol air freshener. When the smell started getting bad, she grabbed that can, opened the lavatory door a crack and sprayed the restroom thoroughly from top to bottom. A second later we heard someone coughing inside the restroom. There was a passenger in there who hadn't locked the lavatory door. That passenger got thoroughly doused with a major amount of air freshener and probably smelled like lilacs clear across the country."

A flight attendant:

"The lavs on a plane always smell bad, and one way we combat the odor is by clipping packets of coffee in the lav, so the place smells like coffee instead of…um….a lav. We always have these coffee packets on hand to brew coffee for the passengers, and we often just slip an extra one into a clip on the wall of the lav, and we try to remember to replace them after a few days with fresh ones, throwing the old ones away. Well, one of those coffee packets had been hanging on the wall a bit too long, I guess. A young lady went into the lav, wearing white hip-hugger pants and a white high-rise top. (I don't know why people wear white when they're traveling.) All of a sudden this packet of coffee disintegrated and coffee grounds rained down upon this woman in her white outfit. She burst out of the lav screeching in alarm

---

…and one toilet for every 11 passengers in first class.

because, when something brown rains down upon you in a bathroom, your first thought is not that it's coffee. It took us quite a while to calm her down and clean her up. We had to work hard to convince her the reason we hang coffee in the lav is to help, and not to terrorize the passengers."

Betty:

"There was a small boy traveling unaccompanied on one of my flights. He was a very young boy and very short—too short to reach up and latch the lock on the lavatory door which also turns on the light. So I told him I would lock the door from the outside, which would also turn on the light for him, and that I would wait outside the door until he was ready to come out again. Well, he'd been in there a few minutes when another flight attendant signaled me that she needed my help with something. So I walked to the front of the plane to help her, and then a passenger asked me for something, and then somebody else distracted me, and soon I had forgotten all about the little boy and went back to doing beverage service. A few minutes later, I heard something peculiar—a noise I couldn't place. The noise kept getting louder, and all of a sudden my heart dropped through my socks as I realized it was the little boy, pounding on the door of the lavatory. I unlocked the door and he came out crying and upset, and I felt so bad that because of me, some kid was probably going to need years of therapy to overcome the trauma of being locked in the lavatory."

An airline mechanic:

"A couple years ago, we were tending an aircraft that had developed a pressurization leak. In order to find the leak, we had to close up the aircraft and then pressurize it. We found the leak and fixed it, but we forgot to de-pressurize the plane. We discovered this later that evening when the maintenance guy who's in charge of emptying the lavatories walked up to us, absolutely covered from head to toe in blue goo and sludge. Seems that when he had opened the valve to empty the septic tanks, all that pressure finally found an outlet."

Betty:

"Sometimes on a plane we have to use our wits to find solutions to problems that arise, just like MacGyver used to on the TV show. One day the first class lavatory door was sticking, and it was sticking really badly, so that one person on the inside had to coordinate with another person on the outside—one pushing, one pulling—in order to get the door open. It was really inconvenient because we had a full flight and there were only three bathrooms on board. What we really needed was some lubricant, but we don't carry any WD-40 on board. So I started thinking of what we had available that would act as a lubricant in a pinch. It was a morning flight, and we had breakfasts to serve, so I wondered if a pat of butter would do the trick. But I didn't want to just spread it on the floor of the bathroom for fear someone would slip, and then we'd have a whole new problem. So I got a maxi pad out of the lav. The lavs usually have maxi pads, and it's amazing how many uses we find for them. I peeled the adhesive strip off and stuck it to the bottom of my shoe. I spread the butter all over the maxi pad, and then used my foot to rub the door jamb back and forth. I kept on rubbing in order to blot up most of the butter. And, sure enough, it did the trick! When we de-planed and a new crew came on board, I told an incoming flight attendant, 'If the door sticks, just put butter on a maxi pad!' and they looked at me like I was nuts. I guess it's not that often that you need to use the phrase, 'Put butter on a maxi pad!'

"When I was laughing over this story to a male flight attendant, he told me he uses maxi pads all the time to catch the drips from the air conditioning units that trickle down through the overhead bins and drip on the passengers. He told me, 'People give me the strangest looks when they see me coming out of the lav with maxi pads in my hands!'

"Then there was the time when I desperately needed to improvise a diaper. Usually when that happens, I look for another parent who's traveling with a baby and ask if they have a spare diaper. This time, there were no other babies on board. So I pulled the synthetic pillowcase off of the disposable pillow and ripped two holes for the legs in the bottom of it. I put a maxi pad in between the leg holes, and it worked really well! Later when a toddler threw up all over himself and his shirt, the parents didn't have any spare clothing with them. So I pulled a pillowcase off the pillow, poked a hole for the head and two for the arms, and that kid looked downright stylish in his pillowcase shirt!"

A pilot:

"One of the things we used to do in the Coast Guard was marine environmental patrols. We were flying a Falcon 200 out of Mobile, Alabama, heading out over the Gulf of Mexico. We were checking for buoy lines and oil spills and carrying a crew of five. Well, our sensor systems operator had a bad case of the runs and was in a lot of discomfort because there weren't any bathrooms on board. The flight commander suggested he use the box that his lunch came in. So the guy removed his lunch and relieved himself into the box. As you can imagine, the odor permeated the aircraft and you can't just roll down a window. So the commander had the brilliant idea to open the drop hatch, which is normally used to drop pumps and rafts and rescue gear to vessels in distress, and toss out the box. So we went down to

---

An average airline toilet uses about 8 ounces (.25 L) of water per flush.

100 feet, ran through the drop check list, opened the hatch, and the dropmaster tossed out the box. But the force of the wind blew the box back inside the plane where it rolled and tumbled and flew all around, spraying poop everywhere. Suddenly all the commander could hear over the intercom system was guys screaming. He says, 'Dropmaster, check in!' and all he heard was screaming. 'Loadmaster, check in!' and all he heard was screaming. He thought men were dying back there. Finally they got the drop hatch closed, but it was such a mess that we had to abort the mission and divert back to Mobile."

very indignant over the state of his baked potato. 'What's wrong with it?' I said. 'Well, just look at it! It's a bad potato! Can't you see how bad this potato is? I want a good potato!' So I picked the potato up, gave it a couple hard slaps while scolding, '*Bad* potato! *Bad* potato!' and then I handed it back to him. 'If this potato gives you any more trouble, you just let me know!'"

The other white meat

One flight attendant, when he ran out of beef and was able to offer only a choice of chicken or chicken, began asking passengers, "Chicken or possum?" When a few adventurous flyers chose the possum, he handed it to them saying, "It tastes like chicken!"

A passenger:

"I was on a flight coming back to the U.S. from Europe. Shortly into the flight there was an announcement that there would be two options for the in-flight meal: a beef dish or a chicken dish. I was listening to my iPod as I saw the flight attendant come down the aisle asking each passenger which dish they wanted. When he got to me

I'll have a diet cherry vanilla coke with whole wheat pretzels.

Honey, this is a 737 not a 7-Eleven!

Airlines and airports recycle only about 20% of their waste.

Food
Follies

I remember when every stand-up comedian had an airline food joke. Now on most flights there is no food at all, or you have to purchase it. Who would have thought that we would miss the good old days...of bad airline food?!

A flight attendant:

"It was a long, late flight from New York to Los Angeles. A l[ot] of the passengers were sleeping, so when I made an announceme[nt] that we were serving snacks, I spoke quietly into the PA mike [so] I wouldn't disturb everyone. I said we had peanuts, cheese a[nd] crackers, granola bars, and Biscoff cookies. I then started servi[ng,] but when I reached one lady and asked her what she wanted [I] had to burst out laughing when she said, 'What the heck—[I'd] like to try some of your pissed-off cookies!' "

A flight attendant:

"I was on a long flight to Hawaii and we were serving ste[ak] and potatoes for dinner. One passenger called me over and [...]

and I saw him ask me (although I couldn't hear him with the iPod on), I replied, 'Chicken!' I saw him look somewhat confused, and I saw his lips repeat the question, so I replied again, louder, 'Chicken!' I now noticed he was trying very hard to keep from bursting out laughing, so I finally took the headphones off to actually listen to his question. It turned out he was not taking meal orders as I had assumed, but was passing out customs forms. He was not saying 'Beef or chicken?' to each passenger, but instead asking, 'American citizen?' Of course, the worst part was that he was French. Now with a smirk and a smooth Parisian accent he said, 'For ze last time, sir, are you an American citizen, or a chicken?'"

A flight attendant:

"I was working a flight from New York to Frankfurt which happened to have Mother Teresa and her entourage aboard. They had bought coach class tickets, but the airline upgraded them to first class at no extra charge, and I was working first class that day. Well, first class on an overseas flight got a full seven-course meal, so I wheeled out the hors d'oeuvres cart, but she didn't want any of that; then I brought out the salad cart, and she had a salad; then I bought out the entrée cart, followed by the cheese and the fruit and so on. Her eyes got really big and she turned to me and said, 'I cannot eat all of this! Young man, what do you do with all the uneaten food from this flight?' and I had to tell her that company regulations dictated that we had to throw it all away. I felt really bad about having to tell her that and I felt like maybe I should get a really big box and collect all the leftover chicken and steak for her. Instead, we ended up taking up a collection among the other passengers on the plane. We raised about $500 for her, and gave that to her instead of a 'to-go' box full of leftovers."

Los Angeles International Airport dumps about 8,000 tons of wasted food annually.

A flight attendant:

"One of my co-workers was working first class when Chet Atkins was aboard. She had just finished serving him his meal when he called her over saying, 'Excuse me miss, I know this sounds like a terrible cliché, but there's a fly in my soup.' She looked, and sure enough, there was a fly in his soup. So she turned to him and said, 'No pets are allowed on this flight!'"

A passenger:

"I was flying on an Australian airline. The flight attendants were picking up trash, and one of them went up the aisle with her trash bag saying, 'Rubbish? Anything I can take off your hands, such as old boyfriends?'"

A Tip From Betty
When we finish serving the passengers and are collecting the trash, it's easy to get the trash from the people in the aisle seats and even from the people in the middle. But collecting the trash from the people in the window seats is much harder because I have to bend over and reach out to get it. This means bending over hundreds of times in a row, especially since I often have three flights on any given day with several hundred passengers each. So it means a lot to me, and really eases the strain on my back, if people will lift up their trash and hand it to me instead of expecting me to bend over and get it. Sometimes the snootier passengers refuse to do this and just wave their hand dismissively at the trash on their seat tray and expect me to collect it for them. When this happens, I will turn to the person next to them, or the person in the next aisle over, and say, 'May I take your trash, please?' After seeing other people lift their trash up and hand it to me, most people generally get the idea. If they still don't get the idea, I just start moving away from them and taking my trash bag with me up the aisle. That's then they finally pick up their trash and wave it at me to get my attention— and that's when I collect their garbage without straining my back.

A flight attendant:

"I was a brand-new flight attendant and it was my very first day on the job. This was back when we still served in-flight meals. It was a short flight out of Denver, only an hour and a half, and every seat was full. It was my job to serve the coach class passengers their meals. Because it was the holidays, we were serving turkey, dressing, sweet potatoes, peas, salad, and a really yummy pumpkin soufflé. And because it was a short flight and a full plane, the other flight attendants told me I was going to have to hurry as fast as I could to get all the meals served on time. So on my first trip down the aisle from the galley to coach class, I was carrying two meal trays. I thought that the doorway that separated first class from coach was wide enough for me and two meal trays. Because I was in such a hurry, I walked into that doorway at full-speed-ahead and it was *not* wide enough for me and two meal trays! I smacked into it so hard that the meal trays bent when they hit the wall, and turkey, dressing, sweet potatoes, peas, salad, and pumpkin soufflé went flying through the air. The soufflé landed on the head of a first class passenger, and his toupee and the soufflé landed on the floor together. I was so horrified that I spent the rest of the flight

I miss the good old days when we served food...and everyone complained about it!

...consecutive plane crashes for the movie *Darling Lili,* at $750 per crash.

locked in the bathroom wondering if I should reconsider my choice of career."

A flight attendant:

"When I answered a call button, a male passenger told me in a very concerned voice that his nuts were swollen. He said I should notify the captain right away. I was a little taken aback, but he didn't expound upon his problem so I figured it must be a 'guy thing' and that the captain would know what to do. So I went to the cockpit and told the captain that a man was complaining about having swollen nuts. The captain was very confused and said, 'Well, does he need medical help? Is he in pain?' I didn't know, so I went back to ask him. 'The captain wants to know if you require the immediate assistance of a doctor.' He looked very perplexed, and then he held up the snack packet that we had handed out earlier, showing me that the foil wrapper was taut and swollen from the change in air pressure. He said, 'My peanuts are swollen and I'm sure that indicates a problem with the cabin pressure, and I thought the captain should know.' When I un-

> **Air treats**
> Otto Schnering, inventor of the Baby Ruth Candy Bar, once promoted the product by hiring a chartered airplane to do a massive Baby Ruth candy bar drop over the city of Pittsburgh in 1923. The ploy worked, and sales took off. Encouraged, he did similar airplane drops in cities in 40 different states and included his new candy bar, the Butterfinger.
>
> During World War II British airmen put ice cream mixtures in cans in the rear compartments, where the plane's vibration combined with the freezing temperatures at high altitudes yielded especially delicious ice cream.

derstood, I burst out laughing, and when he understood what I had misunderstood, he laughed right along with me."

A male flight attendant:

"Years ago the airline I work for used a beverage cart that was very poorly designed. The beverages were stored in drawers, but the drawers were as long as the beverage cart, and they opened from either end. The flight attendant in front of the cart could pull the drawer open, or the flight attendant in back of the cart could pull the drawer open, which made it cumbersome and difficult to coordinate the service. Also, if you weren't careful, you could easily pinch a fellow flight attendant's fingers if you opened your side of the drawer while they still had their hands in it. You had to be sure you could see their hands before opening the drawer, or you had to announce your intention to open the drawer, and of course each person had to open the drawer dozens and dozens of times. Once I was working with a British female flight attendant. I had opened the drawer, and then started rearranging some items on top of the beverage cart while the drawer was still open. To make extra room on top of the cart, I laid a bag of peanuts on top of the open drawer. The other flight attendant, because she could see both my hands, grabbed the drawer to pull it open, at which point I called out, 'Wait! My nuts are stuck in the drawer!' Her eyebrows went sky-high as she turned to me and said in her very proper British accent, 'I beg your pardon?' and I replied, 'Wrong nuts!'"

A male flight attendant:

"I was working the beverage cart starting at the back of the plane and moving forward, and a lady flight attendant was working her beverage cart starting at the front of the plane and moving back, and we met in the middle row of the plane, back to back.

...is the planet's highest commercial airport.

She was serving her final passenger, but she was short a couple packs of peanuts. So she turned to me and asked, 'Do you have two nuts?' and I thought about that for a second before responding, 'Well...Yes.' And she said, 'No, the *other* nuts!'"

A pilot:

"We were about to takeoff when some fun-loving flight attendants decided to put one over on the passengers. They laid a whole bunch of snack packets on the floor of the airplane in the aisle and announced over the P.A. system that they were tired and needed a rest so they were going to deliver the snacks using the easiest method possible. When we took off and banked, the snacks

slid down the aisle all the way to the back, and the passengers picked the packets up off the floor and handed them around. Then one flight attendant picked up the mike and announced, 'OK, pick up your feet because here come the drinks!'"

A flight attendant:

"I was serving on a 767 and on this particular flight about half of the passengers were Buddhist monks, all decked out in their saffron robes. I guess there were about a hundred monks on that flight who happened to be of a particular sect that requires they never take anything directly from the hand of a woman. This was a problem

---

The longest runway in the world is at Edwards Air Force Base in California.
It's 7.5 miles (11.5 km) long.

because we only had one male flight attendant. Thankfully, the monks brought with them a bunch of 'helpers'. The monk would hand the ticket to the helper, the helper would hand the ticket to us, we would check the ticket and hand it back to the helper, and the helper would hand it back to the monk. When we were serving meals, we handed the trays to the helpers and the helpers handed the tray to the monks. Every time we would walk up and down the aisles, the monks would lean into their seats, lest their hand accidentally touch a woman. It was very odd."

A flight attendant:

"There were two young sisters traveling on their own on one of my flights. One was probably about six years old, and her little sister was about four. I was passing out the peanuts and snacks and when I gave the big sister her peanuts she very politely said, 'Thank you, sir!' I then gave a package of peanuts to her little sister. The big sister turned to the little sister and said, 'Now, what do you say to the nice man?' and the little sister stretched out her arm to me with the peanuts in her hand and said, *'Open it!'*"

> *"In America there are two classes of travel:*
> *first class and with children."*
> —Robert Benchley

Dumb Moments &
Stupid Moves

Every time I think I've heard it all, someone surprises me.
People can ask the dumbest questions! And I'm not just
talking about the passengers. Even though flight crews
work above the clouds, we are not above having our own
less than stellar moments. I personally am guilty
of more than my share of stupid moves, but hey,
at least they make good stories!

Betty:

"Occasionally when the doors shut, they don't seal tightly. It's not dangerous when this happens, but it will sometimes cause a high-pitched whine or hissing that can be annoying. When I was a new flight attendant, this happened at the rear door. I went up to tell the pilot about it. He reassured me that his instruments indicated the door was safely closed, even if it was whistling, but he suggested that if I wanted the squeal to stop, I could stuff a lemon in the door. We always carry lemons on board for use in cocktails, so I went to the galley and got a sliced up lemon. Then

I stood in front of the door and tried to figure out what I was supposed to do with the lemon. So I called the pilot and asked him, "What do I do with this lemon?" He laughed and said, "I didn't say *lemon*; I said *linen*. Stuff a linen napkin in the door!"

A pilot:

"On a flight from New York City to Miami, a flight attendant came up to the cockpit and asked me what the large body of water on the left side of the plane was. Thinking she surely must be joking, I told her it was Lake Michigan. She said, 'Oh,' and left. A few minutes later she was back, asking in all seriousness, 'Is that fresh water or salt water?'"

A flight attendant:

"On a flight from San Francisco to Hawaii, a passenger summoned me and asked, 'Are we going to see water the entire way to Hawaii?' and I replied, 'Well, I sure hope so, because if we don't, that means we're not going to Hawaii!' I told her to be certain to alert me if she saw mountains or lakes or anything other than water so I could raise the alarm. She looked out the window, sighed heavily, and said, 'I can't believe we're going to see nothing but water the entire way to Hawaii!'"

Betty:

"One of my sisters called me because she was invited to a wedding in Maui and she wanted to fly to Hawaii for the weekend to attend. She lives in Florida, and I told her the trip would take so long, just getting down there and back, that I didn't think she should go just for a weekend. She thought that was ridiculous, so I helped her make the travel arrangements. There were a bunch of flights just to get from Florida to California, followed by the five-hour flight to

Why do flight attendants have the right to cut off the flow of booze?...

Hawaii. As soon as she got back home, she called me and said, 'It took me so long to get there! Why didn't you tell me it was such a long trip?' I reminded her that I had warned her over and over again. Then she explained to me that as soon as they took off from Los Angeles, she had expected to be landing any minute and simply could not believe how long it took to get there. She had grown up looking at flat maps of the U.S., and on a map in an atlas (instead of a globe), they usually move the Hawaiian Islands right next to California to save space. She thought the Hawaiian Islands were to California what the Florida Keys are to Florida."

Super supersonic
Not realizing that Indianapolis is on Eastern Standard Time and Chicago on Central Standard, a man inquired at the Indianapolis airport about a flight to Chicago. "The next flight to Chicago departs at 1:00 p.m.," the ticket agent said, "and arrives at 1:01 p.m." "Would you mind repeating that, please?" asked the man. The agent repeated the information and then asked, "Would you care to make a reservation?" "No, thank you," he replied, "but I do believe I'll stick around and watch that thing take off!"

A passenger:

"I grew up in Louisiana and I clearly remember the first time I ever flew on a plane. I was flying to Birmingham, Alabama, so the plane had to fly over Louisiana, Mississippi, and Alabama to get there. But I was confused, so I called the flight attendant and asked her, 'Where are the lines?' She didn't understand what I was talking about, so I pointed out the window of the airplane and asked her again, 'Where are the state lines? The state lines that are drawn on all the maps?' I had grown up looking at the state lines on all the geography maps and I thought, right until that very moment, that those lines could actually be seen on the land."

Betty:

"I'm based out of L.A. and, like everything in L.A., the airport is crowded and congested. Because of that, most of the gates are 'tow-in' gates, which means the airplane will land, taxi close to the gate, then shut the engines down and wait for a tug to tow them to the gate. This is to avoid problems with backwash from jet engines. Most pilots have a standard announcement they make so passengers won't get out of their seat while waiting for the tow. One day, right after the captain made his announcement, I heard someone from a few rows back exclaim in disgust: 'Holy crap! I can't believe we made it clear across the country and now we've broken down and have to be towed!' "

A flight attendant:

"Some years ago they invented Braille emergency instructions for blind passengers that explained all the safety features of the plane in raised dots. Shortly afterwards, a handicapped man and his travel companion pre-boarded, and I handed him a Braille emergency book, explaining what it was. He didn't understand, so I ran his fingertips over the dots while explaining it was a Braille instruction manual. That's when his travel companion leaned over and said, 'He's not *blind*. He's *deaf*.' "

A flight attendant:

"My girlfriend was serving on a flight out of Billings, Montana, when the call light kept going off. She walked to the back of the plane to find a businessman who was holding the call button down while speaking into the air vent, saying, 'I would like a Coke and my wife would like a Sprite...' He really thought that was how you placed your order on a plane!"

A pilot:

"We were flying over Meteor Crater in Arizona—a huge hole in the ground left when a meteor slammed into the Earth thousands of years ago. The highway passes the crater, with an access road that leads to the edge of the crater where people can visit a museum and look into the hole. I was reading from a pamphlet that tells all about the crater, and I pointed out the window to show it to a flight attendant. She looked out the window and exclaimed, 'Wow! I can't believe how close it came to hitting that road!'"

A co-pilot:

"Once we had a brand-new flight attendant on board who knew nothing about how to fly a plane. One day in mid-flight on a cross-country trip, she asked the captain how he managed to find his route clear across the country. It just so happened that there was a contrail perfectly outlined below us by the sun and the atmospheric conditions, so the captain pointed at the contrail and said, 'We just follow the lines!' She leaned to the window and looked at the contrail and said, 'What a good idea!'"

> **Twilight zone**
> A passenger on a plane reported seeing a UFO with a yellow light that blinked irregularly while on a flight. He claimed the UFO followed abreast of the plane for the entire flight. Investigators called to the scene found a firefly caught between the two panels of glass in the window where the man had been sitting.

A flight attendant:

"I was working on an L-1011, where the galley is located on the

---

About 435,000 bags are permanently lost in the U.S. annually.

lower level, and whoever is in charge of fixing the meals puts the hot meal cart in the elevator and sends it up to the top level where the passengers are seated. However, on this flight the elevator was out of order. We had a real can-do attitude and wanted to serve the meals in spite of the broken elevator. The only way to do this was to use the emergency escape hatch located under the carpet in the passenger cabin above the galley. We piled cushions and pillows around the hole so no one would accidentally fall in, and then handed each meal tray up though the hole in the floor to another flight attendant who would then run it to the next of the 300 passengers. But wouldn't you know—a drunk guy stumbled up the aisle and ended up falling right through that hole in the floor, landing in the galley below. We were certain we were going to be sued as we picked him up and dusted him off and checked for injuries. But he was just relieved, saying, 'Oh, thank God! I thought I fell through the bottom of the plane!'"

A flight attendant:

"A flight attendant friend of mine drove to the airport on a very hot day. Because his car didn't have air conditioning, he was wearing shorts, a T-shirt, and flip-flops. When he got to the airport, he went into a bathroom to change into his uniform. Suddenly he realized he had forgotten his uniform shoes. He had his suit, his tie, his hat—and no shoes. He had nothing to wear but his flip-flops. He started cursing a blue streak and then stepped out of the stall to discover that a priest was occupying the next stall over. He apologized for his language, and then explained the problem. The priest said, 'I think I might be able to help you!' He pulled out a pair of little black booties that priests wear at the altar. He put these slippers on and you really couldn't tell that he wasn't wearing regulation shoes. The priest happened to be on his

About 4.55 pieces of luggage are misdirected for every 1,000 passengers.

flight, and he was so grateful that he kept plying the priest with free drinks. By the time they arrived in Boston, the priest was so drunk they wheeled him off the flight in a wheelchair. Ever since then, that flight attendant has taken those black booties with him around the world, and he sends the priest a constant stream of photos of the places those booties have been: Here's your booties at the Taj Mahal…Here's your booties at the Eiffel Tower…Here's your booties at the Parthenon…And the priest really appreciates this."

Betty:

"A flight attendant I worked with had long hair, and one morning at the hotel she didn't appear at the appointed hour to catch the shuttle back to the airport to catch our next flight. When we called her room to see what was holding her up, she said she had gotten the curling iron stuck in her hair and she couldn't get it out. We told her to cut the lock of hair off—but she adamantly refused. A few minutes later she came down from her room and climbed into the shuttle with the curling iron stuck into the back of her collar. She worked the entire flight with a curling iron down her neck rather than snip a little bit of hair off."

Betty:

"A flight attendant I worked with was famous for being chronically late. One morning we all met in the hotel lobby to take the van to the airport for our first flight of the day, but she wasn't there. We all thought, 'Here we go again!' and someone called up to her room to see when she was coming down. 'I can't come down—because I can't find my skirt!' She had somehow lost her uniform skirt between the time she took it off the previous evening and the next morning, and she could not find it anywhere.

Approximately 97% of lost bags are returned to their owners within 24 hours.

A couple of flight attendants went up to her room to help her search for it, and they looked high and low, searching every place in that room. Finally they found it, in between the mattress and the box spring. She had placed it there the night before in order to press it, and had completely forgotten about it!"

A flight attendant:

"There was a seven-year-old boy on my flight, flying alone. When he took his seat, I noticed that a very large person had occupied the seat previously and had let the seat belt out to its maximum dimensions. I said to the little boy, 'You should tighten up before we take off,' and I nodded at the seat belt. During take-off as we were climbing, I glanced over at him and saw that he was squeezing his eyes, his arms, his legs and shoulders—everything was as tight as it could be…except for his seat belt."

Crime Busters

• During a skyjacking epidemic, a major airline hired two psychiatrists to act as security agents to screen passengers and arrest anyone who looked suspicious or showed signs of mental instability. Working independently and unknown to each other, the two men had been on the job one day before each arrested the other.

• A pickpocket at the Seville airport had the unfortunate luck to choose the worst possible victim. The thief specialized in international events that drew large crowds of visitors, and he thought he was in his element when he came upon a large group of young men in the airport. He chose his target and dipped into a bag, little realizing he was stealing from Larry Wade, champion 110-meter hurdler for the U.S. athletic team. He was also spotted by Maurice Green, the fastest sprinter on Earth, capable of running 100 meters in 9.79 seconds. According to Darwin Awards (www.DarwinAwards.com), the two athletes quickly chased down the thief despite his hefty head start. The pickpocket attempted to

---

Around 0.005 percent of lost bags are permanently lost.

pretend that he was just an innocent French tourist, but the entire episode was captured on film by a Spanish television crew that had been interviewing Mr. Greene at the time.

• In Knox County, Ohio, a thief broke into a Mooney aircraft and stole the avionics system, including the Emergency Locating Transmitter, or ELT. This device sends out electronic homing signals when a plane crashes. During the robbery, the crook jarred the ELT just enough to activate it, and authorities easily tracked and apprehended the perpetrator.

• Singapore Airline employee Austin Perot figured out how to hack into the computer systems of major airlines and used the knowledge to create fictitious accounts for 29 different fake frequent flyers, putting them 'aboard' various long-haul flights after the plane had already landed. Using this method, he amassed some 17 million frequent flyer miles between 1996 and 2002, enough to fly around the world around 200 times. He used the points to sell discount plane tickets to his friends and family members, before being caught. Perot pleaded guilty—to obtaining financial advantage by deception—in the Melbourne County court.

The San Francisco International Airport handles 60,000 bags daily.

About 480 bags move through O'Hare Airport's computerized
baggage handling system every minute.

Animal
Antics

*Leopards, gorillas, and mice, oh my! Who knew there are
so many airline stories starring our furry friends?
In this chapter we hear about raccoons, dogs, turtles,
squirrels, and mice all flying the friendly skies.
Hang on for a "wild" ride!*

Betty:

"When we boarded late in the evening for a cross-country flight, a man got on with a cat in a carrier. The cat meowed loudly and constantly and would not shut up or calm down. It was a very loud, insistent, annoying meow that never stopped for a single moment. When we took off it was still meowing, and by now the passengers were wondering if they were going to have to listen to this very troubling meowing for the entire five-hour night flight, when everyone was hoping to get some sleep.

"Finally the man came up to me carrying the cat in its cage and he said, 'I know it's against regulations but I was wondering if I could take the cat out of the carrier just for a little while so I can try to calm it down.' He explained that he had just purchased the cat two days earlier and was flying home with it. Under the circumstances, I thought this was a good idea and together we removed the cat.

"Well, it was a very rare and expensive cat, a hybrid that was half Asian leopard, and half domestic cat. It looked like a little leopard and had absolutely huge paws. When I put out my hand to stroke it, it grabbed a hold of my fingers with its paw and held on, just like a little baby will instinctively grab onto a finger. The cat seemed to be comforted by this and quickly quit crying. With the man holding one paw, and me holding the other paw, it eventually fell asleep and the entire plane heaved a sigh of relief. In my career, I've done a whole lot of hand-holding, but this is the first time I've ever held hands with a cat. And a leopard cat, to boot."

A flight attendant:

"A woman was flying with her small dog, which she had checked as baggage. The pilot came on before the flight and told the woman that they were unable to carry the dog in the cargo hold because they were also transporting a large quantity of dry ice, which had the potential of suffocating the dog as it melted, giving off carbon dioxide. The pet carrier was too large to fit under the seat, so the pilot very nicely told the woman that he would carry the dog with him in the cockpit. So this sweet little dog went into the cockpit with the pilot, and he soon regretted his decision.

"It was a long flight, from Atlanta to L.A., and we flight attendants would ring the cockpit to see if they needed anything to drink, or lunch, or whatever. Every time we rang the cockpit, the bell would go 'ding-dong' and it sounded just like a doorbell. That dog yapped his cute little head off every time it sounded. I asked the lady who

About 500,000 animals are shipped by air each year in the U.S.

owned the dog, 'Does your dog bark every time someone rings the doorbell?' and she said, 'Yes, you bet he does!'

"So, having discovered this, we decided we would ring the cockpit every time we thought up a reason. That dog barked his way across the continent, driving the pilot crazy. I'm sure that by the time we arrived in L.A., the captain had quite a headache."

A male flight attendant:

"We were in the middle of a flight and I was walking down the aisle checking on my passengers when I noticed a very large woman (with a very ample bosom) traveling with her pet chihuahua. The chihuahua was out of the carrier and sitting on her lap. Well, I'm a dog person, and I'm sympathetic to other dog people, but rule are rules, and the rule is that animals have to stay in their carriers. So I leaned over to speak to this very large woman (with the very ample bosom) and I explained why the rule is important and why she needed to comply with the rule and put the chihuahua back into the carrier. Without saying a word, she looked at me, and then she looked at the dog, and then this very large woman (with the very ample bosom) picked up the chihuahua and tucked the tiny dog into her very ample bosom. The dog fit there very nicely and seemed very comfortable. So I looked at her, and I looked at the dog (in her very ample bosom) and I said, 'Well, technically, I guess that would qualify as a carrier...' and the dog rode in her very ample bosom for the rest of the flight."

A flight attendant:

"Once a raccoon in a pet carrier was sitting in the luggage loading area, waiting to be put into the cargo hold. The animals are always loaded last, so the people in the area were trying to tempt

---

The Unclaimed Baggage Center in Scottsboro, Alabama, sells about 10 million items from lost luggage annually.

the raccoon with tasty tidbits and morsels to eat. The raccoon wasn't hungry and refused to eat anything it was offered. Then someone stuck a piece of paper in the cage, and the raccoon ripped that piece of paper into tiny shreds, and seemed to really enjoy doing so. This amused the people very much, so they continued to tuck pieces of paper between the bars of the carrier, laughing as the raccoon did his imitation of a paper shredder. Finally the raccoon was loaded on the plane along with all the rest of the luggage. When the plane arrived at its destination, the raccoon was unloaded, and the cargo handlers were dismayed to find that during the flight, the raccoon had amused itself by grabbing every baggage tag it could reach, and ripping them into tiny pieces. The floor of his entire cage was covered in colorful bits of paper that had previously been baggage tags. Needless to say, a lot of suitcases failed to reach their destination on that flight, and the passengers never knew the reason."

A flight attendant:

"Evel Knievel was a passenger on one of my flights years ago. On a hunting trip, he shot a wild turkey, which he then had stuffed. He was afraid it would be damaged if he checked it as baggage, so instead he bought a first-class ticket for his turkey. He got on board with the turkey under his arm, put it in the window seat, strapped it in, and acted as if it was the most normal thing in the world to travel with a turkey. The turkey was the best-behaved passenger on the flight!"

A flight attendant:

"I was working a 777 flight from Phoenix, and as I sat on my jumpseat while we prepared to takeoff, I was directly across from a couple who seemed very nervous. The woman was especially

One of the largest planes is the Boeing 747. If set upright...

fidgety and worried, and kept looking at the ceiling above her head, looking increasingly agitated as we began to taxi to the runway. They kept looking at each other, and then looking at the ceiling, and pretty soon I heard scratching and scraping noises coming from the overhead bin above them. So I asked, 'OK, what's in the overhead bin?' The woman looked embarrassed as she said, 'Flying squirrels!' As soon as she uttered these words, we took off. In a calm voice and with a straight face, I asked her how many flying squirrels were up there. She replied, 'Only four!' She explained that these were her pets and that she was afraid that one was going to harm one of the three others. I then asked what kind of container they were in and she said they were in a backpack, but all in different pockets. I then asked if the airline was aware they were on board and she said no. She explained that the last time they traveled with their pets, they did all the right things. They got the squirrels their required shots, paid the extra money to have carry-on pets and did just fine until their return flight. Apparently Phoenix security wouldn't let them through with the squirrels because they are considered rodents and rodents aren't allowed on any airline. Then this poor couple had to rent a car and drive back to Chicago from Phoenix, forfeiting their purchased airline ticket, all for the love of their pets.

"I said, 'Here is the deal—do not open that overhead bin!' They agreed, and I called the purser to discuss the situation, all the while imagining four flying squirrels escaping and flying through the plane. The purser could hear the scratching noises too, and we decided the best thing to do at this point was to seal off the bin with tape so nobody would open the bin. I sealed the bin while the purser spoke with the Captain.

"We agreed the flight wasn't in any kind of danger, so we decided to proceed to Chicago. When we finally landed, my

---

...it would rise as high as a 20-story building.

instructions were to have these passengers remain seated and make sure the bin with the squirrels was not opened while all the other customers deplaned. Then about 15 supervisors and maintenance workers entered the aircraft and approached us. The workers taped up huge plastic tarps which spanned the full distance between the ceiling and the floor all around the bin. When they opened the bin, three of the four flying squirrels were found in the backpack all in good health, but 'Rocky' was missing. Apparently it took them five hours to find him, finally locating him in another bin halfway down the aisle. The aircraft's next flight was cancelled due to the fact that it took them five hours to find the missing squirrel, plus many hours to inspect all the wires and connections for damage from the squirrel.

"Last thing we heard, the couple was charged with the money the airline lost due to this incident. I can't help but wonder if it wouldn't have been cheaper for them to have chartered a private jet for themselves and their squirrels—or at least to have hired a squirrel sitter and left Rocky and his friends at home."

A pilot:

"As I was doing my pre-flight walk-around, checking the plane before takeoff, I noticed a really big animal carrier that was plainly marked in large letters: 'Do Not Look in the Air Holes.' Of course, that just made me curious so I had to go look in the air holes. Well, there was a large gorilla in there, which I suppose was being transported to a zoo. And he was staring right back out at me through those air holes. What I didn't know was that gorillas interpret direct eye contact as aggression.

Well, everyone else on the tarmac was also reading the signs saying 'Do Not Look in the Air Holes.' and then going over to look in the air holes, so there was a steady procession of bag-

---

The Boeing 747 can weigh up to 875,000 pounds (396,893 kg) fully loaded.

gage handlers and maintenance workers staring in at this gorilla. The gorilla started to get really angry, rocking back and forth in his carrier. You just can't have a moving package on board a plane—especially not one that large. In the end, the gorilla had to be transported by ground, all because of the signs saying '*Do Not Look in the Air Holes.*'"

A flight attendant:

"I was just out of training and my first assignment was from Boston to San Juan. During the flight several passengers in one center section of seats kept getting dripped on. We all assumed it was condensation from the air conditioning system, so we kept wiping it down and trying to keep it from dripping.

"When we landed in San Juan, we arrived at the gate and I went to disarm the doors when I heard a fellow flight attendant start to scream, 'Rats! We've got *rats*!' It turned out that an eccentric woman had placed her two ferrets in an empty overhead bin and they had urinated and defecated all over the bin during our flight. What was dripping on the passengers, and what we were wiping up, was not water, but ferret pee."

A flight attendant:

"A passenger named Greg got a call from his wife when he arrived at the airport for his flight. She was worried because she could not find their cat, Joe, anywhere. It was a large white cat and she said, 'You don't think he might have jumped in your bag while you were packing, do you?' He assured her that was impossible. He'd packed a big duffle bag the previous evening and stuffed it in the trunk of his car, where it had been all night long. He hadn't heard any meowing when he pulled it out or when he checked it. The duffel bag was now in the cargo hold,

---

The Boeing factory is 1/3 of a mile wide, 2/3 of a mile long, and 11 stories tall.

but he didn't think Joe the Cat could possibly be in it. But as the flight got underway, he got to thinking and started getting worried because he had packed the bag in the dark. His friends started teasing him about 'the cat's in the bag' and he made them promise that if he found the cat dead in the duffle bag, that they wouldn't tell his wife but would just help him bury the body in an undisclosed location so she would never know. His flight landed in Los Angeles and he retrieved the duffle from baggage claim, opened it up, and out climbed Joe the Cat, none the worse for the wear—just hungry, thirsty, and a little confused. The bag had gone through X-ray screening at security and apparently nobody noticed a cat skeleton in the bag. Fortunately, Greg had friends in Los Angeles who met him at the airport and took the cat home with them until he could round up a pet carrier and pay the fee to have him flown back home. All his buddies were saying, 'Just stick him back in the bag! It'll be free!' "

A pilot:

"We were flying from Seattle to Pullman in an unpressurized turbo-prop. We had four crates of little white laboratory mice on board destined for the university. Somewhere near Yakima we ran into some turbulence, and one of the crates tipped over, releasing about 20 mice. There were 14 seats on the plane, all of them occupied by college girls on their way back to school after the holiday. There were no cargo doors on the plane, only a curtain, so we could not contain the mice and they ran through the plane. It was an eruption! With the discovery of the first mouse, the screaming started and soon the girls were standing on their seats, hitting the mice with shoes, and the whole scene was complete bedlam!"

A brand new Boeing 777 costs around $165 million.

A flight attendant:

"We were flying from Seattle to San Francisco when we were diverted to Sacramento. We explained to the passengers that there would be an unexpected delay, and that they were welcome to get off the plane in Sacramento, stretch their legs, and re-board after an hour. Everyone on the plane disembarked, with the exception of a blind lady who was traveling with her seeing-eye dog.

"The captain went back to speak to her, asking if she would like to take a walk around. She said no, she was fine, but that her dog would really appreciate a chance to get a little exercise. So the pilot (who happened to be wearing sunglasses) escorted the dog off the plane and walked around the airport and back to the plane again. You have no idea how much people stare when they see a pilot with a seeing-eye dog, especially when he gets on the plane. We had passengers trying to re-book and others wondering if they should abandon ship."

To fill the gas tank on a Boeing 747 requires 45,000 gallons (170,343 L) of fuel.

Safety First,
Laughter After!

*"Ladies and gentlemen, we are here primarily
for your safety." We announce this at the beginning of
every single flight. This is an absolutely a true
and valid statement—but we are not above
having some fun now and again. In this chapter we have
a dead guy, lots of oxygen, and even a visit from
the "Jetway Jesus!"*

Betty:

"Throughout my career I have seen numerous cases of miraculous cures that happen on board an airplane. It has something to do with the airline wheelchairs. People in wheelchairs are always boarded first. Not only do they get on the plane first, but they also get the best spots to stow their luggage. But when we arrive at the destination, people in wheelchairs are always kept until last so they don't hold up everyone else who is disembarking.

"Now, I'm not saying that everyone who orders a wheelchair is faking, but I can't begin to count the times people have boarded the plane in a wheelchair, too sick to walk on their own, but by the time we arrive they've been miraculously cured of their ailment and are among the first to stand up and get off the plane. We attribute this phenomenon to the 'Jetway Jesus'."

A flight attendant:

"On a flight returning to the mainland from Honolulu, a passenger alerted a flight attendant to the fact that something was wrong with the man next to him. The flight attendant checked the guy and realized right away that he was deceased. She got some help from the other flight attendants and they moved the body into the galley, then called for a doctor.

"A doctor on board came forward, checked for a pulse, and pronounced the man dead. So the flight attendant went to the captain and told him one of the passengers had died. The captain said, 'Are you sure that he's dead? Because if he's dead right now, we have to turn around and go back to Honolulu. But if he's dead in about 20 minutes, we can keep going.' So the flight attendant said, 'Let me double check!'

"She went back to the doctor and said, 'Are you in a big hurry to get back?' and the doctor said, 'Well, I have to be back at work

> **Is there a doctor convention on board?**
> When Dorothy Fletcher began having chest pains while flying to her daughter's wedding in Florida, the captain asked if there was a doctor on board. Fifteen people stood up. Dorothy had the good fortune to get sick on board a flight that was carrying heart specialists to a convention in Orlando. She got plenty of attention while waiting for the plane to make an emergency landing in South Carolina. After spending five days in the hospital, she continued on to Florida, where she made it in time for her daughter's wedding.

Air travel is the second safest mode of transportation.
Only the elevator/escalator is safer.

tomorrow.' She said, 'Well, if this passenger is dead now, we have to turn back. But if he's dead in 20 minutes, we can continue on to L.A.' The doctor checked the passenger again and said, 'You know, I think I *do* feel a pulse…'"

Betty:

"One of the things all flight attendants dread is the in-flight medical emergency. When people are stressed, or they forget their medications, even healthy people can become faint.

"I was working a completely full flight with only four flight attendants on board. I was serving meals in first class and had delivered six of them when an elderly man with a pacemaker passed out. Because I was the lead flight attendant, I had to take charge of the situation. I notified the cockpit, asked another flight attendant to get out the portable oxygen tank, began to jockey passengers around to make room for the man to lie down, and paged for a doctor. Fortunately there were two doctors on board, and one of them was a cardiologist.

"Although the man regained consciousness, the cardiologist wanted to hook him up to the defibrillator just to monitor his heartbeat. He also hooked the man up to a blood pressure cuff and started an IV. So now he was attached to an oxygen tank, a defibrillator, a blood pressure cuff and an IV that was hanging from the overhead bin on a coat hanger.

"For me, running back and forth to collect all this equipment, while also keeping the cockpit informed and comforting the sick passenger, was very stressful. With a full flight and only four flight attendants on board, there was no chance we could get the rest of the meals served until the situation was resolved. I made a PA announcement that meal service was temporarily suspended.

"Just when I thought it couldn't possibly get any more stressful,

---

It's recomended that you do not donate blood within 24 hours of flying.

that's when one of the first class passengers, who had received one of the six meals, asked me—in the middle of all this running around—to fetch him another pat of butter for his roll. I couldn't believe that someone could be so callous as to ask me to take time out from dealing with a possible heart attack victim to fetch him an extra pat of butter!

"Then, just in case I needed a little more stress, the man who was hooked up to an oxygen tank, a defibrillator, a blood pressure cuff and an IV, announced that he had to go to the bathroom—so I had to figure out how to get him and all this medical equipment to the lav and back again.

"Fortunately, the doctors concluded that he had suffered from a sudden drop in blood pressure which had caused him to black out, but he was not having a heart attack. He turned out to be fine, but I sure needed a good stiff drink after that."

How do planes fly?

Simply put, it's because air speeds up when it passes over the curved top of a wing. As it speeds up, the air molecules are spread more thinly over the top of the wing. The air molecules on the bottom of the wings are thick. The thinner the air on top, the fewer molecules press against any single point on the wing. The fewer molecules there are pressing down, the lower the pressure.

Patrick Smith describes the science behind flight in his book Ask the Pilot: Everything You Need to Know About Air Travel: "There's also something in Flying 101 known as Bernoulli's Principle, named for Daniel Bernoulli, an eighteenth-century Swiss mathematician who never saw an airplane. When forced through a constriction or across a curved surface, a fluid will accelerate and its pressure will simultaneously decrease. Our fluid is air, which moves faster over the top of the wing, which is curved (less pressure), than it does along the flatter surface below (higher pressure). The resulting upward push contributes to lift."

The two companies of Boeing and Airbus build around 99 percent of passenger jets.

If you hear that a plane is flying 500 mph, it means that this is the speed that the air is traveling over the wings (called "air speed") but this is not necessarily how fast the airplane is moving over the ground (called "ground speed"). If a plane is flying with an airspeed of 500 mph but it is heading into a 50 mph headwind, it will have a ground speed of only 450 mph. But if it's flying with a 50 mph tailwind, it will have a ground speed of 550 mph.

The lift that causes a million-pound airplane to fly is caused by the shape of the wings. If the shape of the wings changes even minutely, the lift is greatly diminished. As little as a half-inch (2.5 cm) of ice on the leading edge of a wing can reduce the lifting power of a plane by as much as 50 percent. So, if you're delayed due to de-icing, don't complain.

A flight attendant:

"A few years ago a friend of mine was on a flight back in the day when we still had the old style of headphones, which were little plastic nubbins that fit in your ears. She answered the call button to find a little old lady who looked just like someone's grandma. She was sitting in her seat with these ear phones stuck up her nose, and she asked the flight attendant why she wasn't getting any oxygen. She had been feeling short of breath and thought this was how they delivered oxygen to passengers."

Betty:

"Every year, all flight attendants have to complete training where we practice emergency procedures. We simulate evacuations and practice shouting commands. One of our commands in event of a crash is, 'Grab ankles! Heads down! Stay low!" and we repeat this over and over as we practice our emergency. One day in Buffalo, New York, the whole crew was in a van on the way to the hotel. There was a really nasty winter storm and the highway was in ter-

---

On October 28, 1929, the first baby to be born in an airplane arrived in a transport plane over Miami. It was a girl.

rible shape. All of a sudden, the van went into a skid, and we did a 360-degree turn, ending up in the median of the highway.

"And all during the entire crash, starting at the moment we began to skid, one of the flight attendants in the van just instinctively started shouting, 'Grab ankles! Heads down! Stay low!' Which just goes to show you that in any emergency, your training will come through."

Duck! It's a Chicken!
The National Research Council of Canada invented a cannon designed to fire dead chickens at speeds of up to 620 mph (998 km/hr). It's designed to test airplane parts that are likely to be struck by flying birds.

A flight attendant:

"We were taking the medical portion of our training when the instructor turned to a new flight attendant and gave her a hypothetical medical emergency to deal with, saying, 'You go to the back of the plane and discover a passenger lying on the floor of the plane, unconscious but breathing. What do you do?' She stared at him with a confused expression on her face as if she didn't understand English, so he repeated himself, 'You go to the back of the plane and discover a passenger lying on the floor of the plane, unconscious but breathing. *What do you do?*' She looked at him blankly and asked, 'What's *butt breathing?*'"

Superman fastens his seat belt
Muhammad Ali got on an airplane but refused to fasten his seat belt when asked by the flight attendant. "Superman don't need no seat belt!" he said. "Superman don't need no airplane, either," replied the flight attendant. Ali fastened the belt.

A co-pilot:

"We were flying from Atlanta to La Guardia, and La Guardia has a curfew, so if you don't arrive

A jet will get about 11 hours of maintenance for every hour it flies.

by a certain time of the evening, you're not allowed to land at all. We had weather issues which delayed our takeoff considerably, so when we finally got into the air, the plane was full of grumpy, irate passengers. No sooner had we taken off than flight control contacted us and said that because we'd been delayed, we were not going to make it to La Guardia on time, and because of their curfew, we'd have to land at JFK airport instead, and bus the passengers to the terminal at La Guardia at 2 A.M.

"Everyone in the cockpit groaned at this news, and nobody wanted to break the news to the angry passengers. The Captain turned to me and said, 'You tell them!' and I replied, 'I'm not going to tell them; *you* tell them!' so we were at a stalemate because we couldn't face the wrath of a plane full of ticked-off New Yorkers. Just at that exact moment, one of our engines failed, and the Captain and I let out a whoop of relief and high-fived each other, saying 'We're not going to New York!' because of course with an engine out, we had to immediately return to Atlanta to have it fixed.

"Instead of informing the passengers they'd be bussed to La Guardia, we made a very serious announcement that we'd lost an engine and were returning immediately to Atlanta. We got back into Atlanta just fine, and all the passengers as they disembarked were congratu-

---

Trust your captain, but fasten your seat belt.

lating us and giving us their blessings instead of cursing and complaining, while the Captain and I were winking at each other and snickering to ourselves. It's probably the only time in history when the people flying the plane were happy to lose an engine."

This might make you feel better
"When a large plane hits turbulence, the passengers don't all feel the same sensations at the same moment. While the passengers in the front may be bumped upward, the passengers in the rear may be bumped downward. Seats in the middle of the plane near the wings, which might be considered to be the fulcrum of a seesaw, often get the smoothest ride. What pilots know but most passengers don't is that airplanes fly just as capably in the midst of turbulence as in smooth, calm air. Turbulence doesn't make the pilots panic or clutch the controls in a desperate effort to control the plane. Turbulence doesn't tear wings off commercial airplanes or shake the fuselage apart. Flying through turbulent air is much the same as steering a powerboat across choppy water. In a boat, passengers expect the thud-thud-thud of the water hitting the bottom of the boat, the rising and falling seesaw of the boat's hull, and the sometimes unexpected drops. Just as boats are strong enough to survive the impact of turbulent water, airplanes are built to withstand turbulent air." –David Blatner in The Flying Book: Everything You've Ever Wondered About Flying on Airplanes *www.TheFlyingBook.com*

When an air cabin is pressurized, it actually expands the aircraft, like a balloon filling with air.

Not exactly

Fifteen minutes into a flight from Los Angeles to Toronto, the captain announced, "Ladies and gentlemen, one of our engines has failed. There is nothing to worry about. Unfortunately, our flight will take an hour longer than scheduled, but we still have three engines left." Thirty minutes later the captain announced, "One more engine has failed and the flight will take an additional two hours. No need to worry, though…we can fly just fine on two engines." An hour later the captain announced, "One more engine has failed and our flight will be delayed yet another three hours. No need to worry, though…we still have one engine left." At that point, a young woman turned to the passenger in the next seat and exclaimed, "Boy, if we lose one more engine we're going to be up here all day!"

A co-pilot:

"As soon as we took off from Nashville, a shaft in a fuel pump broke and one of the engines stopped instantly. We continued to climb so that we could circle around and come back to land at Nashville to get it fixed. Of course, the other engine was carrying the entire burden of the plane, so it was working extra hard to pull us up, which meant it was roaring particularly loudly. I got a call on the intercom from a flight attendant who said, 'Some passengers are complaining that the engine back here is too loud,' to which I responded, 'That's because it's the only engine we have left!' There was dead silence on the line. I guess that wasn't the answer she was hoping for."

Fasten your seat belt!

An average of 58 passengers are hurt each year while flying in the U.S. due to the fact they are not wearing their seat belts during turbulence. It's the leading cause of injury for both passengers and crew.

The speed of sound (Mach 1) was first exceeded in 1947 when Chuck Yeager flew at 697 mph (1,122 km/hr).

A passenger:

"Before a flight from Boston to Washington, D.C., one of the pilots warned us about turbulent air we could expect during our climb and encouraged us to keep our seat belts fastened snugly. The flight was indeed very turbulent, with the plane pitching up and down severely. After one particularly violent drop, and after the plane had stabilized, the pilot came back on, chuckling in his pilot drawl, 'Well, folks, that was quite something. If you weren't wearing your seat belts before, *I bet you are now!*' The plane erupted in complete laughter, which totally diffused the tension we all felt."

Coincidentally Enough...

Bill Eadie wanted more than anything else to play football. He entered Northwestern University of Illinois hoping to make the team. But he was too small and too light, and was heartbroken to find he would never make the grade as a football player. Still, the game fascinated him and he spent every afternoon watching practice, running errands for the coach, and doing favors for the players. Before long he was rewarded with the position of team manager.

"One day, football hero Eddie Rickenbacker called the stadium and Eadie answered the phone. It seemed the game for that afternoon was sold out, and Rickenbacker wondered if Eadie could rustle him up a ticket. Eadie was glad to oblige for such a big name in football. When he delivered the ticket to Rickenbacker, the two men started to talk. "Eadie confessed he was anxious to do something worthwhile with his life after graduation, but he didn't yet know what. Rickenbacker told him to consider going into aviation. Eadie promised to think it over.

"Years later, the plane Rickenbacker was flying in crashed in the Pacific Ocean. He and his companions spent 23 torturous days adrift on the open ocean. Finally a Navy pilot spotted the tiny raft and rescued all who were aboard. The pilot of the rescue plane was none other than Bill Eadie, who had taken Rickenbacker's advice and gone into aviation."

Most airplanes today fly between Mach .80 and Mach .86, which is about 560 mph (901 km/hr).

"Aviation is proof that given the will, we have the capacity to achieve the impossible."—Captain Eddie Rickenbacker

A passenger:

"On a flight from Boston to Florida, which goes over the Atlantic Ocean, I laughed when a flight attendant made this announcement during the safety demonstration: 'In case of a water landing, your seat-bottom cushion can be used as a flotation device. Grasp it at the back, lift it firmly, place your arms through the straps on the underside, and please, take it with you, with our compliments.'"

The reason is...

The reason you have to return your tray table to its upright and locked position is so you won't impale yourself on it if the plane crashes.

The reason you have to return your seat to its upright position is to make evacuation easier in event of a disaster, to minimize whiplash, and to prevent you from slipping under your seat belt in the event of a sudden stop.

The reason you have to turn off your Walkman is so you can hear emergency announcements and instructions.

The reason you have to raise your window shade is so you'll have a better feel for which way is up and which way is down, and give you better orientation if there's an accident, as well as making it easier for rescuers to see inside.

The reason you have to stow your carry-on items and put away your computers is to avoid the possibility of having them act like airborne missiles.

The reason lights are dimmed is so you're not blinded by light while dashing through smoke, and to make emergency lights easier to see.

The Concorde supersonic plane flew at twice the speed of sound, about 1,336 mph (2,150 km/hr).

A passenger:

"Not long after 9/11, when all kinds of new security regulations were being tried out, I was booked on a tiny puddle-jumper to make a connecting flight. There were a grand total of nine passengers on that flight. We were all sitting in the boarding area when the crew made an announcement, saying, 'Good afternoon. We'll be boarding soon. But first, the Federal Government requires that we select two passengers for additional screening on this flight. Would anyone like to volunteer for additional screening?' Two people did volunteer, and I thought it was funny to expect any terrorists who might be on board this teeny-tiny flight to raise their hand and volunteer to be searched."

Sorry, but you can't take that brick with you

In 2006, some 13.7 million confiscated items were collected at U.S. airports. That included 11.6 million lighters. Lotions, gels, and other liquids are taken to the dump, but items such as scissors, knives, large flashlights, snow globes, handcuffs, toy guns, and pointy belt buckles are auctioned on eBay. Bricks, food processors, electric drills, baseball bats, golf clubs, horseshoes, and snow shovels are also among the banned booty. Other items confiscated include a bow and a quiver of arrows, a wooden saber, an old wooden pistol, a realistic-looking plastic grenade, a bottle of perfume shaped like a grenade, a 12-inch (30 cm) metal pipe wrench, a good sized machete, and even a catapult. The State Agency for Surplus Property in Harrisburg, Pennsylvania, sells about two tons of stuff per month, collected from various airports in the northeastern U.S. They've netted over $360,000, and the money is used to fund social programs in Pennsylvania.

The Boeing plant in Everett, Washington, is the world's largest building, if measured by volume rather than area.

Really, really safe

As David Blatner points out in The Flying Book, *if flying were merely 99.99 percent safe, it would result in three fatal air crashes every single day. Flying is actually 99.9999996 percent safe, because only .0000004 percent of planes crash. In fact, more people die in car crashes in the U.S. in six months than have died in all the airplane crashes worldwide over the past century. If flying were merely as safe as driving a car, a jetliner carrying 120 people would crash—with no survivors—every single day of the year. If you choose to drive the distance you're flying rather than take a plane, one study showed that you would be 65 percent more likely to be killed.*

Betty:

"I was flying on a red-eye flight late one night. It was a lightly booked flight so everyone had plenty of room. We dimmed the lights so people could get a little sleep. One man thought he figured out the best way to get a little shut-eye on the red-eye, and he stretched out on the floor by three va-

cant seats. He was positioned with his head lying in the aisle. As I was tending to my duties in the subdued light, I saw something lying in the aisle. I thought it was a piece of trash or a loose item of luggage, so I walked over to pick it up and clear the aisle, only to find it was a man's head, which was attached to a sleeping man.

"I woke him up and explained, 'Someone is going to step on your face! It's kind

---

Disneyland could fit inside the Boeing plant,
with plenty of room for the parking lots.

of an important body part that you don't want to leave in the aisle!'
I told him that if I had been pushing a heavy beverage cart, the cart
would have blocked my view of him and I could have run right over
his head, turning him into an airline version of road kill, which you
might call 'aisle kill'."

A passenger:

"When I was about 15 years old, my entire class took a flight on
a school trip. I was instantly smitten by the pretty girl sitting next to
me. It was a rough flight through a huge thunderstorm, and I offered
to hold her hand as we flew through the lightning bolts.

"I regretted it instantly, because in her panic, she held my hand
tight enough to cut off circulation, and she also dug her fingernails
into my skin, nearly drawing blood. But I was in love, so I bore the
pain silently, while each minute was sheer torture. Unfortunately,
after that flight I never saw her again, and it took a while for my
hand to return to normal."

Problem? No Problem
*After every flight, pilots fill out a form called a gripe sheet,
which lists problems encountered with the aircraft during the
flight that need repair or correction. The mechanics read and
correct the problem, and then respond in writing on the lower
half of the form, stating what remedial action was taken, and
the pilot reviews the gripe sheets before the next flight. Never
let it be said that ground crews and engineers lack a sense of
humor. Here are some actual logged maintenance complaints
and problems as submitted by pilots and the solution recorded
by maintenance engineers.*

Problem: *Left inside main tire almost needs replacement.*
Solution: *Almost replaced left inside main tire.*

The Boeing plant in Everett, Washington, uses as much electricity
as 32,000 homes.

Problem: *Something loose in cockpit.*
Solution: *Something tightened in cockpit.*

Problem: *Evidence of leak on right main landing gear.*
Solution: *Evidence removed.*

Problem: *Dead bugs on windshield.*
Solution: *Live bugs on order.*

Problem: *IFF (Identification Friend or Foe) inoperative.*
Solution: *IFF always inoperative in "off" mode.*

Problem: *Friction locks cause throttle levers to stick.*
Solution: *That's what they're there for.*

Problem: *Engine #3 missing.*
Solution: *After brief search, Engine #3 found on right wing.*

Problem: *Aircraft handles funny.*
Solution: *Aircraft warned to straighten up, fly right, and be serious!*

Problem: *Target Radar hums.*
Solution: *Reprogrammed Target Radar with the lyrics.*

Problem: *Test flight OK, except auto-land very rough.*
Solution: *Auto-land not installed on this aircraft.*

Problem: *Autopilot in altitude-hold mode produces a 200 feet-per-minute descent.*
Solution: *Cannot reproduce problem on ground.*

Problem: *DME [Distance Measuring Equipment] volume un-believably loud.*
Solution: *DME volume set to more believable level.*

Problem: *Mouse in cockpit.*
Solution: *Cat installed.*

The 300 passengers and their luggage account for
less than 10% of the total weight of a 747.

Problem: *Noise coming from under instrument panel. Sounds like a midget pounding on something with a hammer.*
Solution: *Took hammer away from midget.*

"Lady, you want me to answer you if this old airplane is safe to fly? Just how in the world do you think it got to be this old?"—Jim Tavenner

Every commercial aircraft in the world loads passengers from the left side.

Grumps, Grouses & Gripes

*Say you have three flights in one work day.
Each aircraft holds 270 people. That's over 800
passengers to deal with in one day. Is it any wonder that
we deal with the occasional grumpy, stupid, or crazy
person? But you know what the really sad thing is? It's
the grumpy, stupid, and crazy folks that you remember!*

So You Want to Be a Flight Attendant?

Here's how to train for the job:

1. Go to a resale store and find an old, navy-blue suit that an army sergeant might have worn. Add a white shirt and a tie. Wear the same outfit for four consecutive days, every week, all year long. Smile.

2. Go to an airport and watch airplanes take off for several hours. Pretend you are standing by for them and they are all full. Go home. Return to the airport the next day and do the same thing again. Smile.

3. Fill several large boxes with rocks. Lift them over your head and place them on the top shelf of a closet. Slam the door shut until the boxes fit. Do this until you feel a disk slip in your back. Smile.

4. Turn on a radio. Be sure to set it between stations so there is plenty of static. Turn on the vacuum cleaner and garbage disposal. Run them all night. Smile.

5. Remove the covers from several TV entrees. Place them in a hot oven. Leave the food in the oven until it's completely dried out. Remove the hot trays with your bare hands. Serve to your family. Don't include anything for yourself. Eat peanuts. Smile.

6. Serve your family something to drink one hour after you serve them their food. Make them remain in their seats during this time. Ask them to scream at you and complain about the service. Eat peanuts. Smile.

7. Scrounge uneaten rolls off the plates for you to eat two hours later when you're really hungry. Eat peanuts. Smile.

8. Place a straight-backed chair in a closet next to a bathroom, facing a blank wall. Use a belt to strap yourself into it. Eat the stale rolls you saved from your family's meal, preferably while someone is using the bathroom. Smile.

9. Ask your family to use the bathroom as frequently as possible. Tell them to make splashing water a game and see who can leave the most disgusting mess. Clean the bathroom every hour throughout the night. Drink stale coffee in the closet next to the bathroom. Eat peanuts. Smile.

10. Make a narrow aisle between several dining room chairs and randomly scatter your husband's wing-tips and loafers along the way. Turn off the lights and spend the night walking up and down the aisle while banging your shins against the chair legs and tripping over the shoes. Drink several cups of cold, stale coffee to keep yourself awake. Smile.

By one estimation, alcohol is the top leading cause of "air rage." The second leading cause is the cell phone ban.

11. Stay up all night, then wake your family in the morning and serve them a cold, hard sweet roll. Don't forget to smile and wish them a nice day when they leave for work and school. Ask them to berate you. Eat peanuts. Smile.

12. After the family leaves, take a suitcase and go out (preferably in winter) in the yard. If it's not raining, turn on the sprinkling system and stand in the cold and the wet for 30 minutes, pretending you're waiting for the crew bus to pick you up. Then go inside and wait by your bedroom door for another 30 minutes while an imaginary maid cleans and makes up your room. Smile.

13. Change into street clothes and shop for five hours. Pick up carry-out food from a local deli. Go back home. Sit on your bed and eat your meal. Set your alarm for 3 A.M. so you'll be ready for your wake-up call. (It's now 12:30 A.M.) Eat peanuts. Smile.

14. Repeat the above schedule after just three days off, every week for twelve months straight. Now you are ready to become a flight attendant!

Buh bye, goodbye, have a good day, bye now... (Flight crew in training!)

A flight attendant:

"A friend of mine was an attendant on a flight that happened to be carrying a famous person in first class. This person asked my friend to please hang up his coat for him, and my friend replied, 'Just a minute, please!' He then asked him a second time, 'Would

---

Your tolerance for alcohol drops by about 30% when you're at 30,000 feet, so a few drinks will go a long way.

you please hang up my coat for me?' and my friend said, 'In just a minute, please!' At this point the famous person became very indignant and in a very huffy voice said, *Do you know who I am?'* The flight attendant immediately picked up the PA system and made an announcement to the passengers: 'Ladies and gentlemen, does anyone know who this man is? He seems to have forgotten his name.' That did the trick and the passenger didn't say a thing for the rest of the flight."

That's not what I meant, honest!

"The airport in Fresno, California, is a small airport where stairs are pushed to the boarding door and passengers must climb up the steep stairs to enter the aircraft. One day as I stood at the plane's boarding door watching passengers walk across the tarmac, I noticed that the first person coming toward our plane appeared to be furious. She was an ample woman, and her entire body shook as she took each step, as if she were attacking the tarmac. She stomped up the stairs, appeared before me, and said, 'I want to see the captain now! Now!' 'Can I help you?' I said, hoping I could at least diffuse a situation that must have occurred inside the terminal. 'Is something wrong?' 'Yes, and I only want to discuss it with the captain!' When the captain heard the ruckus, he stopped his pre-flight and came out of the cockpit. The angry passenger wasted no time. 'I'd like to report that gate agent,' she stated, pointing to the terminal. 'He was extremely rude. The rudest man I've ever met!' 'What did he do?' asked the captain, grabbing a pen and paper to take notes. The passenger held up her ticket jacket and exclaimed, 'Look at what he wrote on my ticket!' Sure enough, there in big, bold letter, in indelible ink, the agent had written the word "FAT" across the face of her ticket jacket. 'I am so sorry,' I said. 'It stands for Fresno Air Terminal.' I grabbed the ticket from the passenger behind her. 'See? He wrote FAT on everyone's ticket." 'Oh,' said the woman, as she glanced at the other tickets with the word FAT across them. 'Oh.' Then she turned and walked to her seat and never mentioned the incident again.—Flying by the Seat of my Pants by Marsha Marks

It's been estimated that 75% of all in-flight disputes arise from the reclining seat issue.

A passenger:

"My aunt, Velma Maul, was one of the first four stewardesses ever hired by American Airlines back in 1933. Years after her death we discovered a scrapbook she kept of her career with American, including a logbook of her first year of flight (now in the National Air and Space Museum). One of the things that most interested us was an entry where she described the time when Lawrence Tibbett, the famous opera singer, was a passenger on one of her flights. He summoned my aunt to his seat. 'Stewardess!' he said irately, 'I can barely breathe from all the cigarette smoke in this cabin! Can't something be done?' 'Oh, sir,' answered my aunt, 'I'm afraid we can't tell the passengers not to smoke!' It was a different world from today!"

A flight attendant:

"A man boarded an airplane in New Orleans with a box of frozen crabs. A female crew member took the box and promised to put it

---

Here, take this badge and...

According to the book The Smile High Club, *a gate agent endured the ranting and raving of an upset passenger who had problems with his reservation. This passenger shouted and bellowed and everyone in the boarding area witnessed his scathing tirade. The gate agent smiled sympathetically and nodded, and then went to work on the computer and solved the snafu. Then she asked the placated passenger to lean forward so she could pin a special badge on his lapel. "Be sure to show it to the flight attendants when you board," she said. He thought the badge entitled him to special treatment or maybe an upgrade so he pointed it out to the first flight attendant he met on the plane. "Don't I get an upgrade for wearing this badge?" he asked. "Not really," replied the flight attendant. "Normally we put this badge on children traveling alone, to identify the ones needing special attention." Anytime an adult showed up wearing that badge, it was a warning to flight attendants to treat the wearer like a child.*

A study showed that when both men and women are fighting for control of the arm rest, men win about three times as often as women.

in the crew's refrigerator, which she did. The man firmly advised her that he was holding her personally responsible for the crabs staying frozen, and proceeded to rant at her about what would happen if she let them thaw out. She was annoyed by his behavior. Shortly before landing in New York, she announced over the intercom to the entire cabin, 'Would the gentleman who gave me the crabs in New Orleans please raise your hand?' Not one hand went up. So she took the crabs home and ate them herself."

> *"Human behavior is rarely more incomprehensible than when witnessed on an airplane at 30,000 feet."*
> —Elliot Hester, *Plane Insanity*

Betty:

"Because people seated in the exit row might be called upon to open the emergency exit, there are rules governing who gets to sit there. There are only three rules: first, you have to be over 15 years old. Second, you must speak English. Third, you cannot require a seat belt extension. This is because you have to be able to see the exit; you have to be able to verbally direct people to the exit; and you have to be physically capable of opening the exit. This last rule is the most awkward to enforce, because it's really hard to tell people they have to move to a different seat because they're too fat. But people like the exit row because there's extra leg room so sometimes it's hard to get people to move. One day a portly gentleman took his assigned seat in the exit row, and then he called me over and asked me in perfect English if I could give him a seat belt extension. I told him, 'I'm sorry, but you can't sit here if you need a seat belt extension. Let me find you a new seat.' He gave me a blank look and then said, 'No hablo inglés.' Well, that meant he violated two of the three rules of sitting in the exit row, because you can't sit there if you don't speak English, which I told him (in English) while he

---

continued to pretend he didn't understand what I was saying. When I persisted, he then pretended to be asleep. I collected some other flight attendants to back me up, including one who spoke Spanish, and with all of us working on him, we finally got him to move. So take a word from me, and if you're thinking of trying this trick—it doesn't work."

Missing Luggage?

"Getting on a plane, I told the ticket lady, "Send one of my bags to New York, send one to Los Angeles, and send one to Miami!' She said, 'We can't do that!' I told her, 'You did it last week!' "—Henny Youngman

"Someday airlines will offer time travel. You can go to the future year 2090 to visit your progeny, but your luggage will wind up in the Middle Ages."—Frank Romano

A flight attendant:

"I had an overweight passenger in the exit row and I was insisting that he move to a different seat. He was angry about being asked to move and assured me he could open the emergency exit with one arm tied behind his back. Then I told him, 'That's fine, but you have to be able to fit through the window, too!' He finally moved."

A pilot:

"On a packed flight from Fort Lauderdale to La Guardia, we were carrying a full load of New Yorkers. New Yorkers are famous for being cranky and demanding, and they want everything we have to offer. This was back in the day when we handed out souvenir decks of playing cards. We had arrived in New York and I was standing

A study of blinking found that pilots blink less often than co-pilots.

alongside the flight attendants saying good-bye to the passengers when one lady came up the aisle and apologetically handed the lead flight attendant a full air sickness bag as she disembarked. The flight attendant held onto the barf bag with one hand while continuing to tell the other passengers good-bye. Then along came another lady who grabbed the bag out of her hand and said sternly, 'I didn't get one of those!' I made a move to stop her but the flight attendant put her arm across my chest and shot me a look that said, 'Don't you dare!' That lady exited the plane looking very self-satisfied that she managed to get the last of something…even though she didn't know what it was!"

A pilot:

"On a flight from L.A. to Mexico we had a passenger on board who was an illegal alien who was being deported to Mexico. He wasn't a criminal; just an illegal immigrant who was being returned to Mexico. About a half hour into the flight, the flight attendants notified me that this rather odd man was doing something strange: he was sitting quietly in his seat, calmly ripping

> **Memorable airport abbreviations:**
> The abbreviation for Sioux City, Iowa, is SUX.
> Helsinki is HEL
> Damascus, Syria is DAM
> Fukuoka, Japan is…um…never-mind.

Around 18 million people fly on American-based airlines every day. By comparison, the population of New York City (the most populous city in the U.S.) is 8.25 million.

up $5 bills and neatly stashing the pieces in his hat on his tray table. I agreed this was rather weird behavior, but it wasn't destructive or threatening, so I asked them to keep me informed of any developments. A little while later, they notified me again, saying that now this man was completely naked, while remaining quietly in his seat, calmly ripping up $5 bills and neatly stashing the pieces in his hat on his tray table. They had moved all the other passengers away from him, and I agreed that we should return to L.A. to have the man removed from the flight. Everyone thought this guy was crazy, but afterwards I concluded that he was certainly crazy—crazy like a fox, because he didn't get deported after all. At least, not on that day."

A flight attendant:

"I was on a flight when suddenly a very insistent ringing of the call button sent me running to the back of the plane. There I found a very well-dressed professional looking man, his lap full of his briefcase and papers, sitting and pointing out the window. 'There's a little man sitting on the wing of this plane and he's been there for a very long time!' he said. 'Well,' I replied, 'As long as he's out there, and not trying to get in

> ### Tip from Betty
> If your flight is delayed and you get snippy with the flight attendants because, after all, they're getting paid overtime to just sit there—well, guess again! Most flight attendants are paid only from the time a plane pushes back from the gate until it opens its doors at the next city. The most stressful part of every work day—the boarding and the deplaning—is not on the clock for most flight attendants. They don't get paid anything at all if a plane is delayed while the passengers are still in the terminal, and they're paid a fraction of their regular salary if the loaded plane sits on the tarmac for more than an hour. Therefore, flight attendants are just as frustrated at delays as you are.

In 1978 (at the beginning of airline deregulation), 17% of Americans had flown. By the year 2000, 84% of the American population had flown.

here, everything is OK.' I didn't hear a peep out of him the rest of the flight."

You Know You're a Flight Attendant When...

1. You can eat a four course meal standing at the kitchen counter.
2. You search for a button to flush the toilet.
3. You look for the "crew line" at the grocery store.
4. You can pack for a two week trip to Europe in one roll-aboard.
5. All your pens have different hotel names on them.
6. You never unpack.
7. You can recognize pilots by the backs of their heads—but not by their faces.
8. You can tell from 70 yards away if a piece of luggage will fit in the overhead bin.
9. You care about the local news in a city three states away.
10. You can tie a neck scarf 36 ways.
11. You know at least 25 uses for air sickness bags, none of which pertain to vomit.
12. You understand and actually use the 24-hour clock.
13. You own two sets of uniforms: slacks that fit, and skirts that don't.
14. You don't think in "months"—you think in "bid packages."
15. You always point with two fingers.
16. You get a little too excited by certain types of ice.
17. You stand at the front door and politely say, "Buh-bye, thanks, have a nice day" when someone leaves your home.
18. You can make a sentence using all of the following phrases: "At this time," "For your safety," "Feel free," and "As a reminder."

There are more than 750,000 licensed pilots in the U.S.

19. You know what's on the cover of the current issues of *In Touch*, *Star*, and *People* magazines even though you don't subscribe.
20. You stop and inspect every fire extinguisher you pass, just to make sure the "gauge is in the green."
21. Your thighs are covered in bruises from armrests and elbows.
22. You wake up and have to look at the hotel stationery to figure out where you are.
23. You refer to cities by their airport codes.
24. Every time the doorbell rings, you look at the ceiling.
25. You actually understand every item on this list!

> *"Well, aeronautically it was a great success. Socially it left quite a bit to be desired."*—Noel Coward, when asked, "How was your flight?"

Americana

| The beauty queen wave | The game show display | The Flight Attendant two finger point |

NASA once shipped a camera from a space shuttle by air. It got lost and turned up in the Unclaimed Baggage Center.

Due to weather and traffic in the area...we are number 35 in line for takeoff!

The agent can't seem to get the jetway connected

I'm sorry ladies and gentlemen but our entertainment system is not working!

I swear on days like this we should change our slogan to...

We are not happy till you're not happy?!

Ticket to Hell

Early in 2002 Malaysian businessmen did a brisk business selling tickets for flights on the fictitious Hell Airlines. Chinese mourners couldn't buy them fast enough. During the Qing Ming festival, which is a Chinese version of Memorial Day, offerings are burnt to appease deceased relatives. The plane ticket, along with its fake passport, credit card, and checkbook, were purchased by Chinese customers as gifts for their dead loved ones, and delivered by burning.

The captain and the first officer are required by regulation to eat different meals while flying...

Tip from Betty

"One of my pet peeves is when passengers ask me for a pen. Now, you'd think that a pen is a pretty indispensible item, and you'd think that it's easy enough for people to pack a pen whenever they travel. But it seems that at least once per flight, I have to stop whatever I'm doing and fetch someone a pen. The airlines don't supply us with pens to hand out to the passengers and we don't have a secret stash of them hidden away. I often pick up pens at the hotels I stay at and put them in my purse, but that's the only supply of pens available on any flight. When someone asks me for a pen, I have to dig out my purse and find someone a pen. Sometimes I'm just too busy with my duties to do this for people, so I'll say, 'I'm sorry, I've already given out all my pens today.' And a few minutes later I'll notice them digging through their briefcase or their purse or their pockets to find their own pen. So it's not that they are traveling without a pen – it's that they're just too lazy to get their own pen. When you're flying, please bring a pen!"

Congressman, you've been voted out

A gate agent in Washington, D.C., encountered a congressman one day who was deeply involved with a cell phone call. He handed her his ticket and asked her to hold the plane until he was finished with his call, then stood in a corner of the boarding area with his phone glued to his ear, ignoring the boarding calls and refusing to come to the gate when the final boarding call was made. When he finally finished his call and showed up at the gate, he was angry to find that plane had left without him. "How could you do that when I asked you to hold the plane for me?" he bellowed at the ticket agent. According to the book The Smile High Club: Outrageous But True Travel Stories, the gate agent replied, "When the plane was filled, I went on board and told the passengers they were going to participate in good old-fashioned American democracy by getting to vote on the departure time," she said, "One hundred twenty-five of your constituents voted to leave on time. Majority rules!"

...in case some food item is tainted. That way, only one of them will get sick.

Oops! Mishaps, Miscalculations, and Misunderstandings

In a typical day as a flight attendant you better be prepared for whatever gets thrown at you. This chapter includes your airplane leaving without you, dresses and pants falling down, underwear in the aisle, ticking bombs, burning money, and TNT! Just a typical day at work!

A flight attendant:

"A co-worker was pulled aside by security because her bag tested positive for TNT. They searched her bag thoroughly, and all they found was a glycerin suppository. That's how we found out that glycerin suppositories have a chemical make-up similar to TNT. For the rest of the trip, we called her the Blonde Bombshell."

A pilot:

"The story is that William Shatner was scheduled for a flight, and airline officials invited him to use the Crown Room, which is a private club in the airport reserved for upper-crust passengers who pay extra for a membership. Well, some time after that, he was taking another flight, and he went to the Crown Room expecting the same service. This time, however, the attendant had not received any instructions concerning him, and wouldn't let him in. He said, 'But I'm William Shatner!' and got only a blank look in return. 'You know, Captain Kirk!' The attendant turned to him and said, 'I don't care if you are an airline pilot—if you're not a Crown Room member, you're not getting in here!' "

The busiest airports in the world
If the number of aircraft using the facilities is considered, these are the busiest airports in the world:
Hartsfield (Atlanta) (976,447 flights in 2006)
O'Hare (Chicago) (958,643 flights in 2006)
Dallas/Fort Worth (Texas)
Los Angeles (California)
McCarran (Las Vegas)
George Bush (Houston)
Denver (Colorado)
Phoenix (Arizona)
Charles De Gaulle (France)
Philadelphia (Pennsylvania)

If the sheer number of passengers served is considered, these are the top ten busiest airports in the world:
Hartsfield (Atlanta) (82 million passengers in 2007)
O'Hare (Chicago) (70.5 million passengers inn 2007)
London Heathrow (U.K.)
Tokyo (Japan)
Los Angeles (California)
Dallas/Fort Worth (Texas)
Charles de Gaulle (France)
Frankfurt (Germany)
Beijing (China)
Denver (Colorado)

The longest flight in the world is the nonstop flight from New York to Hong Kong, which travels 8,439 (13.581 km) miles...

A flight attendant:

"Jackie Kennedy Onassis flew to Hong Kong to meet her sister Lee Radziwill. They arranged to meet at the airport and then fly out together. They met in the Clipper Club in the airport, which is a private room where the airline treats their upper-class patrons to food, drink, and entertainment while they wait for their flights. Then they discovered there was a problem with Lee's ticket, and someone had to iron out the snafu. Jackie O. asked the agent who was on duty in the Clipper Club for help, but he said that he couldn't leave the Club unattended. Jackie insisted that she was familiar enough with how the Club operated so that she could cover for him while he was gone. So he went with Lee to fix the ticket problem while Jackie greeted guests who came to the Club. I have often wondered what people thought when they entered the Clipper Club to find that their hostess was Jackie Onassis!"

A flight attendant:

"I was on a 747 flight out of Denver with four flight attendants on the plane. One of the flight attendants got off the plane to go check someone's carry-on bag in the cargo hold, and while she was gone, the door closed and we began to taxi out. While we were giving the demo, we looked out the window of the airplane to see the flight attendant running alongside the plane in the snow, waving and yelling and trying to catch up to us. 'Did you notice that we're missing someone?' I said to the other flight attendant. 'Yes, but try to keep it low-key—there's a supervisor on board!' Well, it's hard to keep it low-key when someone is running alongside your plane, waving and screaming. The plane stopped and the air stairs went down so she could get on board, and my co-worker said, 'Tell her to try to be inconspicuous when she gets back on.' Well, she had to walk the entire length of the

---

...over the North Pole in 15 hours and 40 minutes.

plane to get back to her station, and everybody on board broke into applause."

A flight attendant:

"We were flying from Bermuda back to New York and there was a very classy woman sitting in first class. She was wearing a tropical island kind of dress, a wrap-around affair. When we arrived and first class was disembarking, she reached up to get something out of the overhead bin and just at that moment whatever was holding her dress up suddenly let go and the dress landed in a puddle around her feet—and she was not wearing a single stitch of clothing underneath. In a panic she collapsed into her seat and we quickly threw a blanket over her but she sat there mortified until the last passenger had disembarked. By then she had regained her composure, and as she put her dress back on, she told us, 'I guess that's why your mother tells you to always wear underwear.'"

A flight attendant:

"One day I was working a flight and we were busy boarding the 30 or so passengers. I was carrying a bin full of ice to the back of the plane when I was stopped by a rather heavy-set man who was struggling to get his bag into the overhead bin. While he was stretched full-out, reaching upward to the luggage compartment, his belly flattened out. I guess his belt had been cinched around the roundest part of his stomach, because just at that moment his pants fell down and landed on the floor around his ankles. He couldn't reach down to pull them up because he was still trying to shove the bag in, and I was so happy my hands were full of a bin of ice because that absolved me from the responsibility of having to pull his pants up for him. And his underpants were

---

The average American business traveler makes 18.6 trips annually.

ragged and full of holes so they left nothing to the imagination. I guess he didn't listen when his mother told him to wear clean underwear!"

Betty:

"A flight attendant I know had been working a couple of long, hard shifts and she was heading back to her hometown for her days off. When we have days off, we just grab whatever empty seat is available on a plane heading home. So she felt really lucky to get a first class seat home. It was a long flight, and it was night. She thought she would read a little, so she pulled a book out of her bag in the overhead bin. She fell asleep almost right away, and slept for nearly the entire flight. When she woke up, she noticed in the dim light that there was a pair of dirty underwear right in the middle of the first class aisle. She was disgusted and wondered what kind of a slob would put their underwear on the floor in the middle of a plane. Then she looked at them closer and she realized they were *her* underwear—she had accidentally pulled them out of her bag when she got her book out. She grabbed them, hid them, and then spent the rest of the flight pretending to be asleep because she was so embarrassed."

A pilot:

"We were just about to take off when a ramp worker called me and said, 'One of the boxes we were about to load on the plane is ticking, and we don't think we should put it on board. What do you want to do?' I discussed this with the others in the cockpit and we talked it over with the gate agent and the dispatcher. The ramp worker told us the box was labeled with the owner's name, so we decided to have him bring it up to us, and we would have the owner identify it and tell us why it was ticking. So we paged

---

25% of business travelers take a spouse along.

the passenger listed on the box and had her come forward and meet us in the jetway. The passenger was a classic Southern belle, a lovely young lady complete with white gloves and a genteel Southern drawl. She was wearing a crisp skirt and a white blouse and a matching hat, looking for all the world like a debutante at a garden party. When we asked her to open the box and show us why it was ticking, she turned ten shades of red. She opened the box, reached in, and turned off her vibrator. She very primly walked back to her seat, put on her seat belt, dropped her tray table, and put her head down on the table. I think she stayed like that for most of the flight."

A pilot:

"On international flights when we go through security, we often see notices posted and hear announcements made concerning foreign countries that fail to meet American security standards. Once I was going through the security line with a fellow flight attendant when we noticed a poster that said, 'Lima Peru does not meet our security standards.' The flight attendant looked at that announcement, and then turned to me and said, 'That's awful! That's so rude!' and I asked her what she was talking about. She replied, 'Just because some woman didn't make it through security doesn't give them the right to post her name all over the place!' I quietly explained to her that Lima was a city in the country of Peru."

A flight attendant:

"I am not a particularly limber person, but there was one time I accidentally did the splits. It just so happened I was on a 727 when Tommy Lasorda, the former manager of the Los Angeles Dodgers, was in first class, seated directly across from the galley.

The air inside the cabin of a plane is completely replaced with outside air about once every 5 to 10 minutes.

I was working in the galley, wearing high heels and a short skirt, when I slipped on a piece of lettuce on the floor. I skidded half way across the galley floor, hollering all the way, and ended up doing the splits as I went down. Tommy Lasorda toasted me with his beer and said, 'By God, you slide better than half my team!' "

A hair-raising incident

A. Frank Steward, in his book The Plane Truth: Shift Happens at 35,000 Feet, *tells the story of a female flight attendant who wore a very large diamond ring. Because the ring was loose, the diamond constantly swung around to her palm. On one flight, she was serving breakfast when she casually reached over the head of a male passenger to grab something. The diamond ring became entangled in the man's toupee and ripped it off his head. Startled, she thought that some sort of hairy rat-like creature was trying to crawl up her arm. Steward describes the scene:* "She started to scream and wave her hand frantically, but the creature did not jump off. All of the passengers awoke and watched in fear and she screamed down the aisle, waving her hand ferociously. The other flight attendants were in shock as we watched the drama. She made it to the back of Economy and started to hit the wall in an attempt to kill or seriously injure the attacking creature. She eventually stepped on the hairpiece, pulled her hand free, and disappeared into the nearest lavatory. The cabin became silent, as all eyes were on the extremely embarrassed scalpee. He looked like a convertible caught in a rainstorm. Although many tried to hold back their laughter, few were able to. The man promptly reached into his carry-on bag and pulled out a baseball cap and waved to the crowd good-naturedly. The flight attendant emerged from the restroom thirty minutes later, gave an apologetic hug to her victim, and received a round of applause from the cabin. She spoke to him for a while attempting to explain, and surreptitiously handed him a sick bag containing the hairpiece. Before landing, Jean presented the man with a bottle of First Class champagne for being a good sport...She eventually got her ring resized, but never lived down her new nickname of 'Little Running Hair.' "

A typical jet burns 800 gallons (3,028 L) of fuel per hour in flight.

A flight attendant:

"I was working a flight with an attendant who was in charge of keeping track of the cash we collected while selling drinks to the passengers. A lot of money changes hands and there's always a big stack of bills to keep safe. Sometimes, on flights when meals are not being served, the oven will serve as a handy storage spot because you can fit quite a bit of stuff in there. So after we finished serving drinks, this flight attendant looked around for a safe spot to stash the cash and she stuck it in the oven. It would have been okay if only she had remembered to remove the cash bag from the oven after we landed, before the next leg of the flight, because the next flight did serve meals. We turned on the oven to pre-heat it….and all that cash went up in flames. It didn't cause any damage or delay, but we all wept to see so much money go up in smoke."

A pilot:

"I was flying for the Army when we took a plane full of paratroopers over a heavily wooded area of Georgia to practice night jumps. One of the paratroopers landed in a tree and his parachute got tangled in the branches so he could not get down. It was pitch dark and he had no idea how far off the ground he was. When stuck in such a situation, paratroopers are taught to take off their helmet and drop it to the ground while counting, 'One—one thousand; two—one thousand; three—one thousand' and if you can hear your helmet hit the ground by the time you reach four, it's safe to pull out your reserve chute, let it dangle, and climb down it like a rope. But when he dropped his helmet and started counting, he never heard it hit the ground at all, so he figured he was stuck at the top of a very tall tree. The safest thing to do was to wait until morning when he could see what the situation was. Since it was a warm, calm night, he just hung there in his

---

The higher a plane flies, the less fuel it uses because there is less atmospheric resistance where the air is thin.

harness and eventually fell fast asleep. When the searchers came looking for him at dawn, they found him, still sound asleep, with his boots three feet off the ground, and his helmet suspended in the branches of a bush right next to him."

Bad Air Ads

• One airline targeting Hispanic customers designed an ad that boasted about the airline's luxurious leather seats. Unfortunately, the translator didn't quite hit the mark, using a term for "leather" that also denoted a person's hide. The ad came across as saying "fly in the nude."

• In the 1970s, one airline decided to try out a new campaign called "Fly Your Wife Free" in which businessmen were encouraged to bring their wives along at no extra charge. The promotion was so successful that the airline decided to send letters of appreciation to the men who had availed themselves of the service. The letters were mailed directly to their home addresses, where they were opened by the wives. Soon the airline was inundated with letters of outrage from wives who had never heard of the promotion and had never accompanied their husbands on any kind of a free trip. Hundreds of women demanded to know the names of the women their husbands had flown with. The promotion ceased immediately.

• In 1992, sales of Hoover vacuums were lagging in England, so a new sales promotion was rolled out: Buy a vacuum for 100 pounds (approximately $150 at the time) and get two free round-trip tickets to a European destination. Well, customers quickly realized that vacuum cleaners were cheaper than plane tickets, and the vacuum cleaners "flew" off the shelves at a phenomenal rate. The factory had to manufacture vacuum cleaners seven days a week to keep up with the demand. So many people signed up for free plane tickets that Hoover had to charter flights to accommodate them all. The more vacuum cleaners they sold, the more they lost money. The promotion cost the company nearly $50 million.

About 5% of fossil fuels used worldwide each year are used by commercial aviation.

A purser:

"We were on a flight to deliver the plane, and ourselves, to a destination, so there were no passengers on board, only crew members. Somebody decided we should do some 'surfing' on takeoff. To surf, you grab a serving tray, put it on the floor in the aisle at the front of the plane, stand on it, hold onto something solid for dear life, and wait for the moment the plane lifts off from the runway. At that point—when the plane is traveling 140 mph—you let go, and slide clear to the back of the plane on the carpeting. So I decided to give this a try. It would have worked marvelously, too, except that I forgot about the rubber floor in the galley. When the tray hit the rubber, the tray stopped—but I kept on going. That's the last time I ever tried *that*."

A passenger:

"An Australian flight attendant was flying stand-by. When you're flying stand-by, you get a really cheap ticket, but you never know if you're going to get on the plane or not. Generally, you only get a seat if a paying passenger fails to show up. If you're seated on a plane when the paying passenger shows up, you get booted off the plane again. So this flight attendant named Mr. Gay was flying stand-by, and he was called to board the plane. After being seated, another passenger asked if he would switch seats, so he agreed. Then, the paying passenger showed up at the last minute. So the ticket agent boarded and went to the seat that was supposed to be occupied by Mr. Gay, and said to the man sitting there, 'If you're Gay, you'll have to leave the plane.' The real Mr. Gay overheard and stood up to say, 'He's not Gay. I'm Gay, and I'll leave the plane.' Then a passenger a few rows back got all huffy and indignant and stood up shouting, 'I'm gay, too, and by God, you're never going to kick *me* off the plane!'"

The exhaust blast behind a 747 jet engine causes a 150 mph (241 km/hr) wind.

A pilot:

"A friend of mine was a flight attendant on a flight out of Salt Lake City. It was late at night and the plane wasn't scheduled to board for another hour and a half. So she decided to take a nap on board the plane while she waited. The problem was that the ship cleaners were busy vacuuming and tidying up, and they kept disturbing her. So she opened one of the closets and took her blanket and pillow in there, shutting the door behind her and curling up on the floor. Well, she fell very deeply asleep and when it came time to board, nobody could find her. The crew finally decided they had to leave without her. She didn't wake up until the plane was pushing back. She did the only thing she could do—she adjusted her clothes, smoothed her hair, and tried to step elegantly out of the closet as if it were the most normal and natural thing in the world to do. Not a single passenger said a word—but it took a long time for her fellow flight attendants to stop razzing her about it."

> **Marma from heaven**
> Two cartons of Dickinson's Fancy Sweet Marmalade fell through the windshield of Kitty Wolf's car as she drove by Newark International Airport. It was later determined that a catering service had stacked the cartons of jam on the landing gear and then forgotten about them.

> *"The airport runway is the most important mainstreet in any town."*—Norm Crabtree, aviation director for Ohio

A baggage handler:

"At the airport where I work, people buy their ticket and check in at one station, and then they bring their suitcases over to my station to check their bags. It's customary for us to take the luggage from travelers, check their tickets, and say back to them, 'That's three bags to Chicago' or 'That's one bag to Miami' so that we're

---

Larger planes such as a 777 will burn 2,000 gallons (7,571 L) per hour.

sure we get the luggage tagged with the correct destination. One day two little old ladies came up to my station, on their way to Las Vegas. They each had one suitcase. I took their suitcases from them and said, 'That's two bags to Vegas.' They got offended and said, 'What?' I began laughing as they sputtered and protested, 'How dare you call us bags!'"

A flight attendant:

"Years ago, in the days before they invented jetways, we all hated the flight to Fairbanks, Alaska, in the winter because we had to stand by the open door of the plane on the runway and wait for the passengers to board. It wasn't too bad for the male flight attendants, but

When your bags are permanently lost, airlines are required by law to compensate you at the rate of $9.07 per pound of lost luggage...

the women flight attendants were wearing their regulation skirts, which were very cold in sub-zero temperatures, and their regulation shoes, which were pointy patent leather pumps. Their feet would be freezing by the time the passengers were aboard. So one day they decided to turn on the galley oven and warm up their shoes before boarding. Unfortunately, they either turned the temperature up too high, or left their shoes in there too long. When they went to take them out, the leather had shrunk and the toes of their shoes had curled up and back, so they looked exactly like genie shoes. They didn't have any other shoes with them, so they ended up wearing genie shoes on the entire flight. At least their feet were warm."

Tip from Betty

"Passengers sometimes get confused when they see flight attendants on board that are not lifting a finger or doing anything at all.

This is because we are 'dead-heading' which is when we're just flying home for our days off, or we're flying to another airport to pick up another flight we're scheduled for. Often times, we're still in our uniforms, but we're not on duty. This drives some people nuts. On one such flight, I was sitting in the middle seat with a passenger on either side of me, when a lady across the *aisle kept giving me the evil-eye, glaring at me the entire time. Evidently, she thought I was the laziest flight attendant ever. Finally she stood up and, with her hands on her hips, said, 'Would you at least get me a blanket?' I explained to her I wasn't on duty, and since she was standing up already and I was trapped by two passengers, it would be easier for her to get the blanket herself. So take it from me, if you see a flight attendant reading a magazine and sipping a drink or taking a snooze, they're not being lazy—they are just dead-heading."*

When your bags are permanently lost, airlines are required by law to compensate you at the rate of $9.07/pound ($20 per kg), which works out to about $180 for a 20-pound bag.

Cockpit
Comedians

In general people easily accept colorful behavior from a flight attendant. But they have a different perception of an airline pilot. Our pilots are highly trained individuals, and they are truly the cream of the crop. I have the utmost confidence in their flying abilities, but people may be surprised to hear that pilots can also be colorful and zany. Every once in a while you run into a pilot who is slightly off the beaten runway. In this chapter we have cockpit competitiveness, a pretty-boy pilot, a lightning bolt strike and zany pilot announcements.

> *How do you know when a date with a pilot is half over? It's when he says, "Okay, enough talk about flying and airlines. Now let's talk about me."*

A flight attendant:

"Occasionally it will happen that the pilot will forget to turn off the microphone when he finishes making his announcements, and the entire plane full of passengers will overhear what's going on in the cockpit until the mike is switched off. This happened once, and the passengers heard as the pilot turned to the co-pilot and said, 'I could really go for a rare steak, a strong coffee, and a hot young woman!' Mortified, a flight attendant went racing up the aisle to tell the pilot to turn off the mike. A passenger watched her rush by and called out, *'Don't forget the coffee!'* "

A pilot:

"On a flight from Dallas to Honolulu, a flight attendant knocked on the cockpit door and handed the co-pilot a camcorder, saying, 'I know you guys aren't supposed to do this, but could you get some film of the islands as we're on our way in?' The co-pilot agreed, and he started filming the islands, naming them off and making a few comments about the flight. When he panned the camera around the cockpit, there was the pilot standing on his seat with his pants around his ankles, giving the camera a full moon. The co-pilot got a really nice long shot of the moon, and handed the camcorder back to the flight attendant when they landed without saying anything. That night over dinner and a few beers, the pilot and co-pilot had a lot of laughs over the incident, and then they started thinking up more things they could do with that camera. So the next day as they were flying out, heading back to Dallas, they asked the flight attendant if they could have her camcorder to do some more filming for her. 'Oh,' she said, 'That wasn't my camera. That was a passenger's camera!' "

A pilot:

"There's always a kind of competitiveness between pilots regarding what kind of a plane you're flying, what kind of equipment you've got, and who you're flying with. At one time there was an F-16 pilot who came across a C-130 droning across the sky. So the

---

About 10% of commercial pilots worldwide are female.

F-16 pilot got on the same frequency as the C-130 and said, 'Hey, watch this!' Then he did a barrel roll and a couple of loops, and said to the C-130, 'Top that!' The C-130 pilot said, 'Well, actually, I can do something that's way better than that. Just you watch.' And the C-130 just kept on chugging across the sky. After waiting about ten minutes, the F-16 pilot got back on the radio and said, 'What are you going to do?' and the C-130 pilot said, 'I've already done it! I got up, went to the back of the plane, got my lunch, went to the bathroom, poured a cup of coffee, and came back to the flight deck!' "

A flight attendant:

"New hire flight attendants have six to eight weeks of training, and new hire pilots have eight to ten weeks of training. In the

In 1970, 1% of business travelers were female.

lunch room one day, I overheard an exchange between a new flight attendant and a pilot. The flight attendant said, 'Well, if I had known that it was only two more weeks of training, I would have been a pilot!'"

A pilot:

"A friend of mine was a brand new flight attendant and she was still pretty nervous about the job and worried she'd screw up somehow. One day she was on a DC-9 when the pilot and co-pilot both asked her to bring them some coffee. She went and fixed two cups of coffee and then went back to the cockpit. Just as she opened the cockpit door and reached in to hand them their coffees, the plane hit some turbulence and both of the cups went flying out of her hand. There was coffee everywhere—running down the windshield, all over the instruments, dripping from the ceiling. The image that is forever burned into her memory is the

Ladies and Gentlemen, we are beginning our initial descent into the Portland area.

The temperature is 50 degrees with broken clouds...but we will try to have them fixed before we land!

By 2000, 51% of business travelers were female.

co-pilot turning to face her with a single drip of coffee hanging off the end of his nose. She never lived it down."

A passenger:

"A few years ago there was a flight approaching Glasgow airport in Scotland. The captain was on the speaker and the announcement went something like: 'Good afternoon ladies and gentlemen. We have just started our approach to Glasgow and will be landing in about 20 minutes and OH, MY GOD!!!' The mike suddenly went dead. There was complete silence in the passenger cabin. A few minutes later the announcement continued: 'Hello again, ladies and gentlemen. Sorry about that! Just as I was speaking to you, the stewardess was handing me a cup of coffee which spilled into my lap. You should see the front of my trousers!' A voice piped up from one of the passengers: 'That's nothing! You should see the *back* of mine!'"

A co-pilot:

"I was working for a small regional airline. Because the cockpit tended to stay hot inside, it was outfitted with a small fan. The fan was not protected by a cage or anything, but the blades were made of rubber. If you accidentally stuck your hand in the fan when it was on, it would make a horrible noise, and the smack on your hands would be a terrible jolt. You'd jerk your hand back, thinking you'd certainly lost some fingers—but no damage would be done. One time I was flying with a pilot who obsessively ran his hands through his hair. He was constantly combing his hair with his fingers. When we leveled off, he said he was going to make an announcement to the passengers. He picked up the mike and said, 'Ladies and gentlemen, this is the Captain speaking....' and then he ran his hand through his hair,

About 650 million people travel on U.S. airlines annually, and there are over 100,000 flight attendants to serve them.

and his hand hit the fan and it made this terrible splatting noise. With the mike still keyed, he shouted all kinds of obscenities at the top of his lungs before he dropped the mike. There was a long moment of silence. Then the call light dinged and the flight attendant wanted to know what was going on. We explained it to her and she said, 'Well, you better make an announcement right away because you've got a plane full of people who think we're all about to die!'"

A first officer:

"A few years ago I was flying with a captain who was famous for being a character. We were getting ready to push back from the gate in London. At the time, the runway was undergoing repairs and there was a lot of construction going on as they worked to fix the pavement. So the captain got on the PA system and made an announcement, saying, 'Folks, I want you to know that they're doing a lot of work on the runway pavement, so we might have a little bit of a rough takeoff. I just want you to know that it's not the pilot's fault; it's not the airplane's fault; it's the *asphalt.*'"

> **This is your captain speaking: Don't have a cow, man!**
> A. Frank Steward tells of the time that Nancy Cartwright, who does the voice of Bart Simpson, was onboard a flight he was on. She was invited to the cockpit to make all of the captain's announcements, which put the entire plane into hysterics.

A flight engineer:

"I flew a regular route with a regular crew to Salt Lake City that always took us right over the top of the Grand Teton Mountains in Wyoming. The Captain would always point out the mountain range to the passengers as we flew over. One day the

---

The average air temperature outside the plane at 35,000 feet (10.7 km) is about 60 degrees below zero F. (-49 degrees C).

co-pilot told the Captain that next time we flew over the Tetons, he should tell the passengers where the name of the mountain range originated. The Captain said he wouldn't touch that with a ten-foot pole. I asked him why not, and he said it was far too risky. I said that was ridiculous, and it was nothing to be embarrassed about or ashamed of, so he invited me to make the announcement when we went over the Tetons. I picked up the mike and said, 'Ladies and gentlemen, we are now passing over the Grand Teton Mountain range of Wyoming. These 14,000 foot-tall mountains were first explored by French fur trappers who gave them their name. They must have been lonely for female companionship, because 'teton' is the French word for 'breast', so Grand Tetons actually means 'big breasts.' However, it must have been quite a long while since they'd seen a woman, because, as you can see, there are *three* major peaks in the Teton range!' I then hung up the mike. Within seconds, every single flight attendant was

Pilot Sayings

• *Always try to keep the number of your landings equal to the number of your takeoffs.*

• *There are three simple rules for making a smooth landing. Unfortunately, no one knows what they are.*

• *You know you've landed with your wheels up if it takes full power to taxi to the ramp.*

• *The three most useless things to a pilot are the altitude above you, the runway behind you, and a tenth of a second ago.*

• *The propeller is just a big fan in front of the plane that's used to keep the pilot cool. If the propeller stops, the pilot starts sweating.*

• *Truly superior pilots are those who use their superior judgment to avoid those situations where they might have to use their superior skills.*

Nigeria Airways wanted to update their image. The first thing they did was change their logo from an elephant to an eagle.

crowding the cockpit saying, 'We can't believe you just said that!' I began to worry I'd get in trouble after all, and I asked if the passengers were offended. 'Are you kidding?' they said. 'The plane is full of French Canadians! They *loved* it!'"

A pilot:

"When I was the second officer on a long flight, I came on the PA system every so often in order to point out interesting views and mention interesting facts. I pointed out mountain ranges and lakes; I pointed out things on the right of the plane and features on the left of the plane; I told them what the weather was like where we were going and what time we would be arriving. After we landed, I was standing in the doorway saying goodbye and everyone was thanking me for a nice flight. Then two little old ladies toddled up to me. One blue-haired lady said, 'Oh, I appreciated your tour guide information so much! I just loved hearing about all the things we were seeing! Thank you for keeping us so well informed!' I was flattered and told her, 'You're very welcome!' But then her blue-haired companion tottered up and said, 'As for me, I just wished you would shut up!'"

> **The flying Smiths**
> *Some years back, a plane was preparing for takeoff at La Guardia field. The captain was Clifford Smith; the First Officer was Harry Smith; the Second Officer was Ben Smith; the purser was Julie Smith; and the stewardess was Priscilla Smith.*

A flight attendant:

"When gas prices went so high that it sent the price of flying spiraling upwards, suddenly fewer and fewer people were flying. On one flight where there were a lot of empty seats, the pilot got

---

The average jet has about 3 million parts, which are held together by about 3 million fasteners.

on the P.A. and said, 'Ladies and gentleman, as we prepare to taxi down the runway, I'd like to request that if there's an unoccupied window seat next to you, please move over to that seat so that the other airlines think we're full as we go by.' "

A pilot:

"A pilot in training saw a bright blinking light in the night sky in front of her as she flew, and she thought it was air traffic heading for her. She kept asking for clearance to fly higher and higher to avoid it. When her instructor asked her why she kept moving higher, she pointed at the light and said she needed to fly above it. He looked at it and said, 'Do you really think you can fly higher than Venus?!' "

A pilot:

"For years the mandatory retirement age for pilots was 60—no exceptions made. One pilot I know of never mentioned this to his wife because he had a girlfriend in another city. When he reached the age of 60, he retired without ever telling her, while he kept making trips across the country to see his sweetie. When he got home, he'd tell his wife all about the piloting he'd done. Well, this scheme worked for him right up until the day his wife went out to coffee with some other pilots' wives. One of them asked her, 'So, how's your husband enjoying retirement?' She said that he wasn't retired. 'But didn't he turn 60?' 'Yes, but he didn't retire, he's still flying!' They all turned to her and told her the mandatory retirement age was 60—no exceptions. Well, that was the end of *that* wife! I don't know about the girlfriend.' "

A pilot:

"A friend of mine was a pilot with twelve years of experience, but he flew one day with another pilot who seemed to feel my

---

The weight of the paint required to cover a jet adds between 400 and 1,000 pounds (181-453 kg) to the weight of the aircraft, depending on the size.

friend needed a lot of coaching. Whatever he was doing, it wasn't quite right, and the other guy was constantly giving him advice which he didn't need or appreciate: 'I think you should slow down a little more'; 'You should lower your flaps now'; 'You should begin your descent here.' After a little bit of this, when it became obvious that it wasn't going to stop, my friend pulled out a little notebook and a pen and started taking notes every time some unneeded advice was offered. So when his co-pilot said, 'I think you should slow down,' he'd pull out the notebook, jot a note, and put the notebook back in his pocket. 'You should lower your flaps' and he'd whip out the notebook and write something down. 'You should begin your descent here' and out would come the notebook. Finally, he got up to use the bathroom but he left the notebook lying on his seat. The other guy was curious to know what he'd been writing down, so he picked it up and looked through it. All that it said was, 'Screw you. Screw you. Screw you' all over the paper. So he put the notebook back where he found it, and didn't say another word for the entire day."

A passenger:

"Due to a mechanical problem, followed by a weather delay, followed by a traffic jam on the tarmac, our flight was four hours late in leaving. When we finally arrived at our destination, tired and grumpy, the captain made this announcement as we taxied towards the terminal: 'On behalf of this airline and the entire crew, we want to thank you for flying with us today. We realize that you have a choice in selecting your air carrier, and we hope next time you think of an on-time departure you'll choose us anyway.' All the tension in the cabin evaporated, and the passengers were smiling as they deplaned."

---

110 million cubic yards of dirt was moved to construct
Denver International Airport...

A pilot:

"When I was a young pilot, we had a full flight and were flying from Atlanta to New York when we encountered several huge ugly thunderstorms. We were given clearance to fly through the middle of a couple of the biggest thunderclouds. When we were right in between them, the plane was hit by a huge bolt of lightning. It made a big bang—an ear-splitting explosion—but it didn't harm the plane in the least. I made a PA announcement telling the passengers what had happened; and then we continued our flight. When everything had calmed down, the co-pilot asked me if I had heard the blood-curdling scream that followed the lightning strike. I had been so focused on my duties that I hadn't heard it, but the co-pilot heard it and he wondered which of the passengers had screamed that loudly. When we landed, one of the first class

Lightning strikes
Almost every single day, an airplane somewhere is hit by lightning while flying. The last time a plane crashed because of lightning was in 1963. Today, all planes have 'static wicks' along the rear edges of wings. These metal wicks collect electrical energy—not only lightning but also static charges—and dissipate them harmlessly in the air behind the plane. Even when lightning strikes the fuselage, the passengers are insulated from any contact with the electrical charge.

passengers lagged behind. It turned out he was a million-mile passenger, and he asked to have a word with me after everyone had exited the plane. He congratulated me on how the incident had been handled and remarked on how calm everyone had stayed—with the exception of that one huge horrendous scream. 'Yes,' I replied, 'my co-pilot heard that scream and wondered if it unnerved the other passengers.' The man said, 'Well it did indeed unnerve the other passengers, but not because of the scream as much as the person who was doing the screaming.' I asked him who it was and he replied, 'Your lead flight attendant.'"

A female pilot:

"A couple years back I was flying a 727 with an all-female crew. We were sitting at the gate waiting to push back when a male passenger boarded and stuck his head in the cockpit. He saw first one, then two, then three women and he exclaimed, 'Wow! Look at all the women up there!' Quick as a flash, the second officer turned around and said to him, 'And we're not afraid to stop and ask directions, either!'"

Famous Bail Outs

• In 1959, a military pilot name Col. Rankin bailed out of his single engine plane when the engine failed at 46,000 feet (14,020 m). A storm was in progress over the Carolina coast at the time, and he went right through the middle of it. It would normally take a man 13 minutes to fall 46,000 feet, but Col. Rankin got caught in the updrafts and came to earth 45 minutes later. Fortunately, his parachute opened at 10,000 feet (3,048 m) and he landed intact. A passing motorist took him to the hospital, where he was found to be suffering from frostbite and shock.

• In 1955, Pilot George Smith ejected from his disabled plane. That wouldn't have been so bad, except that George was in a F100A Super Sabre jet fighter flying at 777 mph (1,250 km/hr) at 35,000 feet (10,668 m). Thus, he became the first person ever to bail out while traveling faster than the speed of sound. His clothing was torn to pieces, and his socks, helmet, and oxygen mask ripped off. He experienced a deceleration force of 40 G's, meaning that he weighed an equivalent of 40 times his weight. He was unconscious when he landed in the ocean off the coast of California. By some miracle, he landed right next to a boat and they rescued him. He was in a coma for a week and spent the next six months in the hospital.

There are more than 200,000 airplanes registered in the U.S. including military, private, and commercial.

- In 1942 Lt. I. M. Chisov of Russia had to bail out of his damaged plane without a parachute. He fell 21,980 feet (6,699 m), landed on a steep, snow-covered mountainside, and slid to the bottom. His pelvis was broken and his spine injured, but he survived and recovered.
- During World War I, Captain J. H. Hedley was in a plane over Germany when the aircraft took a hit. Hedley was sucked out of the plane at 10,000 feet (3,048 m). The pilot of the plane took evasive action by plummeting in a vertical dive. When the plane pulled out of the dive, Hedley landed unhurt on the tail. He hung on till the plane was brought safely to a landing.

Memorable Milestones in Aviation History/Herstory

1910: Baroness Raymonde de Laroche of France became the first licensed female pilot. Upon receiving her license, she said, "Flying is the best possible thing for women."

1921: Bessie Coleman became the first American black female pilot. She had to go to France to learn how to fly because Americans would not instruct a black woman. "I refused to take no for an answer," she said. Later she started a flying school. "I decided blacks should not have to experience the difficulties I had faced, so I decided to open a flying school and teach other black women to fly."

1930: Ellen Church became the first female flight attendant, convincing Boeing that having women aboard was the perfect thing to calm nervous male passengers. Previously, the co-pilots or "cabin boys" were responsible for serving passengers.

1951: Carlene Roberts was elected vice president of American Airlines, Inc., becoming the first woman to hold such a high-ranking office in the airline industry.

1953: Jacqueline Cochrane became the first woman to fly faster than the speed of sound. She piloted an F-86 Sabrejet over California at an average speed of 652.337 mph (1,049 km/hr).

The Boeing 747 averages about 0.16 miles per gallon, (0.07 km/L) but since it's carrying 200 or so people, it's getting three times better gas mileage per passenger than an average SUV.

1958: Ruth Carol Taylor became the first black woman to become a flight attendant, making her initial flight on Mohawk Airlines from Ithaca, NY to New York City.

1973: Bonnie Tiburzi became the first female pilot hired by a major carrier when she went to work for American Airlines. She later said, "In the early days, they said I was trying to make a statement, but I was trying to make a living."

1986: The first all-female flight occurred when Captain Beverly Bass, co-pilot Terry Claridge, and flight engineer Tracy Prior embarked on an American flight from Washington, D.C., to Dallas/Fort Worth, TX. Each wore a red rose in her lapel to signify the first flight in aviation history to have an all-female crew.

Speaking of women pilots
"Flying is a man's job and its worries are a man's worries."
—Antoine de Saint-Exupery

"Women will never be as successful in aviation as men. They have not the right kind of nerve."
— Hilda Hewlet, the first English lady to fly solo

"Women must try to do things as men have tried. When they fail, their failure must be but a challenge to others."
—Amelia Earhart

"Women do get more glory than men for comparable feats. But, also, women get more notoriety when they crash."
—Amelia Earhart

"No. I just wanted to fly airplanes."
—Lt. Col. Jackie Parker, when asked if she pursued her flying career because she viewed herself as blazing trails for other women. She was the first woman in the U.S to be assigned to an F-16 fighter squadron.

A Boeing 747 prepared for a long flight may carry as much as 30,000 lbs. ...

"I'm an Air Force officer first, a pilot second, and then Nicole. The female part is last...My job is to be the best right wingman that I can be."
—Captain Nicole Malachowski, first female pilot with the Thunderbirds, the United States Air Force flight demonstration team

"My daughter just thinks that all moms fly the space shuttle."
—Air Force Col. Eileen Collins,
first female U.S. space shuttle commander, 1999

"It is now possible for a flight attendant to get a pilot pregnant."
—Richard J. Ferris, President, United Airlines

... (13,608 kg) of fuel at takeoff. A gallon of fuel weighs 6.7 pounds (3 kg).

The Last Word

Betty:

Well, that's about it for this book of crazy airline stories. I hope you have enjoyed the ride through the sky as much as I have. When I travel to foreign countries my favorite thing to do is to get to know the locals. I try to learn and understand how their world is like or unlike my own. The airline world is like its own country, with its own rules and language and culture. It's a world that I still feel privileged to be a part of. Maybe after reading this book, you can feel like you've gotten to know the locals (your flight crew) a little better.

If luck is on my side I'd like to put together another book. So if you have any of your own airline stories, you can send them to bettyinthesky@gmail.com and maybe you can be part of the next Betty book!

If you want to hear new airline stories you can always hear me and my pilot and flight attendant friends on my podcast at bettyinthesky.com or in iTunes. I hope you will join me for my next episode...so we can travel the world together!

Happy flying!

Betty!

MMMmmm... the airplanes are full of well dressed civilized passengers...we still serve hot meals...the pilots are all tall dark and handsome...we still stay at glamourous hotels...and most importantly...people start calling me a stewardess again!

Betty was born the youngest of ten children in Pittsburgh, Pennsylvania. She knew from a young age that she wanted to travel and see the world. After graduating from Shippensburg University, she got a job as a flight attendant for a major airline. Betty currently lives in Los Angeles, California and is still flying—so you might see her on your next flight!

Even turtles don't watch the safety demonstration!

In September 2006 she started her own podcast called "Betty in the Sky with a Suitcase." Composed of airline and travel stories, the podcast is reminiscent of an old fashioned radio show, giving listeners an insider's view of life in the air.

You can find more information at www.BettyInTheSky.com.

Janet Spencer is known as the Trivia Queen of the Universe, the Royal Ruler of Useless Information, the Master of Arcane Knowledge and Extraneous Lore, the Keeper of Forgotten Facts and Startling Statistics. She began her trivial career in 1987 when she started a weekly newsletter called *Tidbits*. After running that for nearly a decade, she wrote for a company called Trivia Time for six years; spent two years as a staff writer for *Uncle John's Bathroom Reader*; and then published a book called *Montana Trivia* with Riverbend Publishing. That was followed by *Yellowstone Trivia*. Her next book project will be published in 2010. Called *Quick Quirks*, it's an addictive set of trivia quiz questions. Find Janet's books at RiverbendPublishing.com or TriviaQueen.com.

Bye now,
Bye now...
you should be
off the plane
BY NOW!!